WING AND TRAP SHOOTING

A CLASSIC HANDBOOK ON MARKSMANSHIP AND TIPS AND TRICKS FOR HUNTING UPLAND GAME BIRDS AND WATERFOWL

BY **CHARLES ASKINS**
ORIGINALLY PUBLISHED IN 1910

LEGACY EDITION

THE CLASSIC OUTING HANDBOOKS COLLECTION
BOOK 13

FEATURING
REMASTERED CLASSIC WORKS OF THE HIGHEST QUALITY FROM **THE TIMELESS MASTERS AND TEACHERS** OF TRADITIONAL HANDCRAFTS AND OUTDOORS SKILLS

Doublebit Press

New content, introduction, cover design, and annotations Copyright © 2020 by Doublebit Press. All rights reserved.

Doublebit Press is an imprint of Eagle Nest Press www.doublebitpress.com | Cherry, IL, USA

Originally published in 1910 by Charles Askins.

This title, along with other Doublebit Press books are available at a volume discount for youth groups, outdoors clubs, craft groups, or reading groups. Contact us at info@doublebitpress.com for more information.

Doublebit Press Legacy Edition ISBNs Hardcover: 978-1-64389-170-5 Paperback: 978-1-64389-171-2

Part of the Classic Outing Handbooks Collection: Book 13

Disclaimer: Because of its age and historic context, this text could contain content on present-day inappropriate outdoors activities, outdated medical information, unsafe chemical and mechanical processes, or culturally and racially insensitive content. Doublebit Press, or its employees, authors, and other affiliates, assume no liability for any actions performed by readers or any damages that might be related to information contained in this book. This text has been published for historical study and for personal literary enrichment toward the goal of the preservation of American outdoors and handcraft history and heritage.

First Doublebit Press Legacy Edition Printing, 2020

INTRODUCTION
To The Doublebit Press Legacy Edition

The old experts of the woods, mountains, and farm country life taught timeless principles and skills for decades. Through their books, the old experts offered rich descriptions of the outdoor world and encouraged learning through personal experiences in nature. Over the last 125 years, handcrafts, artisanal works, outdoors activities, and our experiences with nature have substantially changed. Many things have gotten simpler as equipment and processes have improved, and life outside, on the farm, or on the trail now brings with it many of the same comforts enjoyed in town. In addition, some activities of the old days are now no longer in vogue, or are even outright considered inappropriate or illegal. However, despite many of the positive changes in handcrafting, traditional skills, and outdoors methods that have occurred over the years, *there are many other skills and much knowledge that are at risk of being lost* that should never be forgotten.

By publishing Legacy Editions of classic texts on handcrafts, artisanal skills, nature lore, survival, and outdoors and camping life, it is our goal at Doublebit Press to do what we can to preserve and share the works from forgotten teachers that form the cornerstone of the authentic and hard-wrought American tradition of self-sustainability and self-reliance. Through remastered reprint editions of timeless classics of traditional crafts, classic methods, and outdoor recreation, perhaps we can regain some of this lost knowledge for future generations.

On the frontier, folks made virtually everything by hand. Old farmers' knowledge and homestead skills were passed on to the future generation because it meant survival. In addition, much of traditional handcrafts and outdoors life knowledge was passed on from American Indians – the original handcrafters and outdoorsmen of the Americas.

Today, much of the handcrafted items of the frontier are made in factories, only briefly seeing a human during the process (if at all). Making things by hand indeed takes much (often strenuous) work, but it provides an extreme sense of pride in the finished job. Instantly, all hand-made items come with a story on their creation. Most importantly, though, making items with traditional methods gives you experience and knowledge of how things work.

This is similar to the case of camping and the modern outdoors experience, with neatly arranged campsites at public campgrounds and camping gear that has been meticulously improved and tested in both the lab and the field. These changes have also caused us to lose this traditional knowledge, having it buried in the latest high-tech iteration of your latest camp gadget.

Many modern conveniences are only a brief trek away, with many parks, campgrounds, and even forests having easy-access roads, convenience stores, and even cell phone signal. In some ways, it is much easier to camp and go outdoors today, and that is a good thing! We should not be miserable when we go outside — lovers of the outdoors know the essential restorative capability that the woods can have on the body, mind, and soul. But to experience it, you need to not be surrounded by modern high-tech robotic coffee pots, tents that build themselves, or watches that tell you how to do everything!

Although things have gotten easier on us in the 21st Century when it comes to handcrafts and the outdoors, it certainly does not mean that we should forget the foundations of technical skills, artisanal production, and outdoors lore. All of the modern tools and cool gizmos that make our lives easier are all founded on principles of traditional methods that the old masters knew well and taught to those who would listen. We just have to look deeply into the design of our modern gadgets and factories to see the original methods and traditional skills at play.

Every woods master and artisan had their own curriculum or thought some things were more important than others. The old masters also taught common things in slightly different ways or did things differently than others. That's what makes each of the experts different and worth reading. There's no universal way of doing something, especially today. Learning to go about something differently helps with mastery or learn a new skill altogether. Basically, you learn intimately how things work, giving you great skill with adapting and being flexible when the need arises.

Again, to use the metaphor from the above paragraphs, traditional skills mastery consists of learning the basic building blocks of how and why the old artisans made things, how they lived outdoors, and why woods and nature lore mattered. Everything is intertwined, and doing it by hand increases your knowledge of this complex network. Each master goes about describing these building blocks differently or shows a different aspect of them.

Therefore, we have decided to publish this Legacy Edition reprint in our collection of traditional handcraft and outdoors life classics. This book is an important contribution to the early American traditional skills and outdoors literature, and has important historical and collector value toward preserving the American tradition of self-sufficiency and artisan production. The knowledge it holds is an invaluable reference for practicing outdoors skills and hand craft methods. Its chapters thoroughly discuss some of the essential building blocks of knowledge that are fundamental but may have been forgotten as equipment gets fancier and technology gets smarter. In short, this book was chosen for Legacy Edition printing because much of the basic skills and knowledge it contains has been forgotten or put to the wayside in trade for more modern conveniences and methods.

Although the editors at Doublebit Press are thrilled to have comfortable experiences in the woods and love our modern equipment for making cool hand-made projects, we are also realizing that the basic skills taught by the old masters are more essential than ever as our culture becomes more and more hooked on digital stuff. We don't want to risk forgetting the important steps, skills, or building blocks involved with each step of traditional methods. Sometimes, *there's no substitute for just doing something on your own, by hand.* Sometimes, to truly learn something is to *just do it by hand.* The Legacy Edition series represents the essential contributions to the American handcraft and outdoors tradition by the great experts.

With technology playing a major role in everyday life, sometimes we need to take a step back in time to find those basic building blocks used for gaining mastery – the things that we have luckily not completely lost and has been recorded in books over the last two centuries. These skills aren't forgotten, they've just been shelved. *It's time to unshelve them once again and reclaim the lost knowledge of self-sufficiency.*

Based on this commitment to preserving our outdoors and handcraft heritage, we have taken great pride in publishing this book as a complete original work without any editorial changes or revisions. We hope it is worthy of both study and collection by handcrafters and outdoors folk in the modern era and to fulfill its status as a Legacy Edition by passing along to the libraries of future generations.

Unlike many other low-resolution photocopy reproductions of classic books that are common on the market, this Legacy Edition does not simply place poor photography of old texts on our pages and use error-prone optical scanning or computer-generated text. We want our work to speak for itself and reflect the quality demanded by our customers who spend their hard-earned money. With this in mind, each Legacy Edition book that has been chosen for publication is carefully remastered from original print books, *with the Doublebit Legacy Edition printed and laid out in the exact way that it was presented at its original publication.* Our Legacy Edition books are inspired by the original covers of first-edition texts, embracing the beauty that is in both the simplicity and sometimes ornate decoration of vintage and antique books. We want provide a beautiful, memorable experience that is as true to the original text as best as possible, but with the aid of modern technology to make as meaningful a reading experience as possible for books that are typically over a century old.

Because of its age and because it is presented in its original form, the book may contain misspellings, inking errors, and other print blemishes that were common for the age. However, these are exactly the things that we feel give the book its character, which we preserved in this Legacy Edition. During digitization, we did our best to ensure that each illustration in the text was clean and sharp with the least amount of loss from being copied and digitized as possible. Full-page plate illustrations are presented as they were found, often including the extra blank page that was often behind a plate and plate pagination. For the covers, we use the original cover design as our template to give the book its original feel. We are sure you'll appreciate the fine touches and attention to detail that your Legacy Edition has to offer.

For traditional handcrafters and outdoors enthusiasts who demand the best from their equipment, this Doublebit Press Legacy Edition reprint was made with you in mind. Both important and minor details have equally both been accounted for by our publishing staff, down to the cover, font, layout, and images. It is the goal of Doublebit Legacy Edition series to preserve America's handcrafting and outdoors heritage, but also be cherished as collectible pieces, worthy of collection in any person's library and that can be passed to future generations.

Every book selected to be in this series offers unique views and instruction on important skills, advice, tips, tidbits, anecdotes, stories, and experiences that will enrich the repertoire of any person looking to learn the skills it contains. To learn the most basic building blocks leads to mastery of all its aspects.

WING AND TRAP SHOOTING

WING AND TRAP SHOOTING

BY
CHARLES ASKINS
AUTHOR OF "THE AMERICAN SHOTGUN."

Illustrated with Diagrams

NEW YORK
OUTING PUBLISHING COMPANY
MCMXI

COPYRIGHT, 1910, BY
OUTING PUBLISHING COMPANY

COPYRIGHT, 1911, BY
OUTING PUBLISHING COMPANY.

CONTENTS

CHAPTER	PAGE
I. Wing-Shooting Problems	9
II. "Aiming" the Gun	21
III. Snap-Shooting, Deliberate Swing and Rapid Swing	41
IV. Primary Lessons	57
V. Some Shooting Psychology	73
VI. Speed of Flight and Where to Hold	91
VII. Hints on Shooting Different Game Birds	108
VIII. Clay Bird Shooting	137
IX. Field Etiquette	155

ILLUSTRATIONS

	PAGE
Gun-Pointing—With Both Eyes Open—	28
Three Ten-Shot Targets Made with a 22 Rifle at 20 Yards with a Blinder Over the Rear Sight, Showing Effect of Binocular Gun Pointing	39
Rough Snap, Semi-Snap and Rapid Swing	42
The Difference in Lead Between a Snap Shot and a Swinging Shoot	50
Estimating Distance to Hold Ahead in Lengths of the Bird	105
Arrangement of Firing Points in Reference to Traps	145
How Distance Handicaps May Be Measured at the Firing Points	147

CHAPTER I

WING-SHOOTING PROBLEMS

IN wing-shooting an object in motion must be struck by missiles from an arm also in motion. The whole science of wing-shooting consists in delivering a charge of shot, not directly at the flying target, but to a point where the bird will be when the charge reaches it. A woman novelist states the matter very naively when telling her sister sportswomen how to shoot English sparrows with a 22 rifle. Incidentally the lady cleverly demonstrates that she possesses all those qualities of lively imagination so requisite in a writer of "fiction for girls." According to the authoress she early discovered that when attempting to hit the little birds while they were sitting she missed because of their springing away with the flash of the gun, but when she jumped them and shot *where they would be when the bullet got there*, she killed them every time. Wing-shooting is as simple as that, merely shoot exactly where the bird will be when the shot gets there and success is certain, even with a rifle.

Many of us have had more trouble to do this with a shotgun, however, than this feminine writer of fiction seems to have found with a rifle, hence this book on the science of wing-shooting. If the birds invariably flew in the same direction with a motion as even as the flight of an arrow, at one unvarying rate of speed, and the gunner knew how to gauge the speed and angle to the fraction of an inch, possessing at the same time the mechanical regularity of a machine in every movement he made, I see no reason why he should not be as successful as the lady.

In field shooting every separate shot may afford its own individual problem which must be solved instantly if the game is to be killed. Wing-shooting problems are highly complex, moreover, because nearly every factor is unknown. The only factor, indeed, that is absolutely known, or should be, is that when the gun is held right the bird is killed. The death of the bird proves, *per se*, that the problem was correctly solved, and there is no other correct solution. Reasoning backward from results we know that the mind stated the unknown factors with truth and reckoned from them without error. However, suppose the bird were missed, the question then is to learn which of the unknown factors was misstated, **and** here our difficulties begin.

It reminds me of a department in an old arithmetic of my father's which was called supposition. You supposed such and such to be the case, and this governed a second unknown quantity, which finally led to solving the problem, provided your first supposition had been correct; otherwise you tried again—in wing-shooting at another bird.

The unknown factors in wing-shooting are the behavior of the shot charge and where it has gone when you miss; the direction, rate of speed, and evenness of flight of the target; the mechanical ability of the gunner to perform certain acts with absolute regularity and precision; the behavior of the shooter's mind and nerves under varying degrees of tension.

If only one of these unknown quantities were known, fixed, and stable, it would immensely facilitate learning to shoot on the wing. For instance, if our shot charge went up to the target in the shape of an immense black ball, thirty inches in diameter, that we could see strike or miss the target, we could all learn more of this art in a year than we now do in a lifetime. The expert shot can frequently tell why he has missed and where his charge went, but not so the novice for whom we are writing. Even the most experienced are frequently puzzled as to the cause of missing, though in their case it merely adds to the fascination of the game which would lose in interest if made too easy.

In the same way if we could shoot at game which had an undeviating line of flight, with angles that never changed and a speed that never varied, striking the mark would be greatly simplified. We would then have conditions similar to those that govern trapshooting with artificial birds where high scores are made with such regularity as to become monotonous.

Given a shot charge that could be seen and a target at known angles whose rate of flight never changed, and we would still have two unstable factors to contend with, the inability to make a perfect machine of the human body and poor team work on the part of brain and nerves. Mechanically nature has endowed us differently. A man may be able to draw one straight line, but if you tell him to draw ten, one of them will be crooked; some other can draw ten straight lines, but will fail before reaching a hundred. The more difficult the task and the longer continued, the higher the degree of mechanical skill required. An expert modern trapshot is simply a great mechanic and nothing else, but a high degree of mechanical skill is a requisite in every description of wing-shooting. Nevertheless it is only *one* of

WING-SHOOTING PROBLEMS 13

the factors that lead to success in live bird shooting.

The action of an individual mind and nerves under varying degrees of excitement is one of the shooting factors that are extremely hard to control. Reliable work can be accomplished only by the man whose mind and nerves have been trained to that very sort of thing. They must work with automatic rapidity, without effort, under all circumstances. Pulling the three-pound trigger of a shotgun is a very simple thing but it takes one man six times as long to accomplish it as it does another, or the trigger may be pressed in 4-100 of a second ordinarily but under excitement will be pulled in 1-100 of a second. If one pull places the charge upon the bird the other would probably miss it.

It might be well to illustrate some of the shooting principles mentioned. A quail is passing the gun at a distance of twenty yards and the arm is aligned two feet ahead of the bird and fired, resulting in a kill. Now the student of wing-shooting has an apparent foundation to work upon, one of his unknown factors has become a fixed quantity; a bird crossing at right angles, twenty yards distant, can be killed by holding two feet in advance. But the next bird that affords a similar shot is a duck and shooting two feet in front of it scores a clean miss. His theory of holding two feet ahead of the target proved wrong in this case and he must find reasons. By and by it may occur to him that the duck was flying faster than the quail, forty feet a second faster. The necessity of closely calculating the speed of flight of the target is thus strongly impressed, and it dawns upon him that one of the unknown factors, speed of flight, can never become a fixed quantity, but must always be estimated, and upon his sound judgment depends his growth of skill as a shot.

The next duck that comes along he leads four feet and kills, much to his satisfaction, for now he knows that two feet in advance of a quail will kill it and four feet in front will connect with ducks. However, a third duck is of a different variety, one that comes loitering by at twenty miles an hour. A pull four feet ahead of this fowl results in another rank miss and a badly puzzled shooter. Holding two or four feet in advance doesn't all depend on the variety of bird for the same wings can carry it fast or slow, and every bird must be judged individually.

Again a quail comes by. A two-feet lead will surely kill it as it did before, but just as the trigger is pressed the bird suddenly swoops, and the charge goes harmlessly above it. Birds must

WING-SHOOTING PROBLEMS

fly evenly if our novice is to strike them; yes, and anyone else—that is what the second barrel is for. Yet another duck wings by and the gunner means to try that four foot lead again, but the aim is high. He knows it, but there is no time for more than the one aim and he cannot avoid throwing his charge away. Our tyro has learned something else, though; if he is to kill he must have the mechanical ability to place his charge exactly where he means it to go, otherwise the knowledge of speed and where to hold that he has been acquiring is all wasted.

More opportunities occur and the student resolves to be extremely careful as to where he places his next shot. All his movements are more deliberate. He swings slowly and pulls steadily and carefully, as nearly as he can judge exactly four feet ahead of the duck, but it goes on without the loss of a feather. Now what the deuce was wrong? Did he fail to estimate the speed, or to hold where he intended? He may not know it or learn what was the trouble for a long time, but the miss was due entirely to his extreme care and overcaution, to dwelling on the trigger and taking 6-100 of a second to pull, in place of his usual 1-100. During the time lost by his over carefulness the bird flew four feet and the shot passed away behind. His finger and brain worked together like balky horses; when one lunged forward the other held back.

Gradually, he acquires knowledge, but all birds do not fly past at twenty yards. A big bird swings down upon him and he thinks it very close, but the usual lead fails to cut a feather. His gun swung to the very spot he wished, he pulled in exact time, the flight of the fowl never wavered from a straight line, and yet he missed. Neither would he ever have known why except for a friend standing near who asked him where he had held and how far off he considered the bird to be. His reply was twenty-five yards and he had held five feet in front of the old drake. He was skeptical when told that the fowl was not less than forty-five yards distant and that he should have aimed from eight to ten feet in front of it instead of five.

All this will be dwelt upon later. Here I wish merely to impress upon the reader that the difficulties of wing-shooting lie almost entirely in the inability of the gunner to detect the cause of error. Should he ascribe the trouble to one thing and it proves to be something else, he will surely go farther astray. There is no such thing as profiting by our mistakes unless we know what those mistakes are. A bird might be missed by giving it too much lead while the shooter, concluding he had not led enough, would get farther and farther out with every succeeding miss.

Very likely the result of a perfect estimate of distance, angle, and speed is thrown away by the novice keeping poor time, swinging too fast or too slow, with a consequent placing of the charge elsewhere than where he thinks he did. Under such circumstances the most natural and easiest thing to do is to change the point of aim with the inevitable additional misses that are as certain to follow as that two wrongs do not make a right.

A false diagnosis leads to the novice swallowing many bitter and useless doses. It is like a hunter hurrying to camp but on the wrong road, the faster he walks the farther off he gets; he ought to learn the right road by traveling it often enough.

Some of the problems of wing-shooting are much more complex than any of the foregoing. It took the writer a good ten years of steady practice to solve one, and he thinks well of his work at that.

Through years of shooting I was considerably exercised by the fact that I missed easy shots, generally quail going straight away or gently quartering—shots that should have been as easy as falling off a log. Very often this happened when I was perfectly cool and collected, covering my target with such ease and certainty that missing should have been impossible. By and by, from being told by companions and seeing the shot strike the water or sand, I learned that the trouble was shooting low. There was no doubt that I missed by shooting under, but I couldn't see why when the bird had been quivering along just above the muzzle of my gun as it had a thousand times before when killed. One thing was obvious; I only lost the birds that I felt sure of killing, those that were covered with deliberate, calculating accuracy.

That being the case, I had only to quicken time, or shoot a trifle more recklessly to kill, and this I could do. However, this did not satisfy me; I wished to know reasons for the miss as the only sure means of preventing its recurrence. My first conclusion was that with deliberate shots I flinched and dropped the muzzle without knowing it. This satisfied me in a way, though I worried because I never could detect the flinching or discover means of preventing it. Then I solved the mystery though I still miss the birds sometimes.

Here is the solution which applied in my case and might or might not in others. At the exact instant when an experienced shot expects his weapon to be discharged, he unconsciously leans forward to catch the recoil which would otherwise throw him backward out of balance, preventing the quick delivery of his second barrel. Now suppose the weapon misses fire, there being no recoil to restore the equilibrium of the body, it continues forward and if the gunner is standing in a light duck boat he may be pitched out. On firm ground the muscles of the feet will quickly restore him to position, but he will find his gun pointing well beneath the target.

In a minor degree all this happened to me when I pulled deliberately. Leaning forward to catch the kick which did not come at the anticipated time because of slow pulling, down went the muzzle of my gun enough to insure a miss. Of course leaning forward might not depress the muzzle of the gun if you did it consciously, but not one shooter in a thousand knows that he does it, and considerable poor work can be attributed to this cause.

Close observation, experience, and practice will take you safely over the road to the expert wing-shot's camp, and the farther you travel the smoother the path becomes—only do not take the wrong trail or walk in a circle, neither trust anyone else to more than point the direction you ought to go.

In an entire day's field shooting no two shots

may be alike; indeed it is a question if two shots are ever exactly similar in live bird shooting. One bird is driving, another is coming in; this little chap quarters with a rising flight, and the next is dropping like a bullet; the snipe dodges, while the mallard swerves and towers; now a wary old pintail beats up against the wind and hovers over the decoys, but forty yards beyond a blue wing teal whistles down the wind at a hundred and twenty miles an hour. No man ever lived or ever will live that could kill them all, which is as it should be.

I can remember the time when I could recall every kill made during an entire season and where I held for the shot. That time will never come to me again. The very best sport is enjoyed only by the ambitious novice who is just beginning to learn. Youth, a good gun, and the brown birds rising in the rag weed field need ask no odds of king or millionaire. What matter if in five only one solved problem has deadly results, life is before the boy and the skill that is surely coming to every man who loves the gun.

CHAPTER II

"AIMING" THE GUN

WING-SHOOTING is of comparatively modern origin. A hundred years ago very few birds were killed awing, and those with a long-barreled old flintlock that usually had double sights and was fired with what we should consider a slow, pottering aim. Wing-shooting really dates from the invention of percussion caps in a practical form, about 1830, and the present style of shotgun shooting is of very modern origin.

Naturally the rifle method of aiming had its influence for a good many years, a full half century in fact, long after the invention of breech-loading guns. The old manner of shooting a shotgun was to close one eye and squint low over the breech, theoretically never pulling trigger until the front bead was accurately aligned upon the target. Many an old veteran still speaks learnedly of "drawing a bead" on the game. The author's wing-shooting career has been connected with the breechloader only, yet in his first lessons, given by his father, the necessity of closing one eye if any accuracy of aim were to be attained was strongly emphasized.

In truth the primer of gun-firing was to learn to close one eye instantly and invariably, preparatory to aiming, and the second principle was not to shut them both before pulling the trigger. If in those days any man had discovered that he could kill game by simply pointing his gun without closing his eye or seeing a sight, he would never have had courage enough openly to advocate such a system of gun aiming.

Doubtless the coming of nitro powder has had much to do with the development of our present slap-bang fashion of shotgun shooting, yet due credit should be given to Doctor Carver who is properly entitled to be called the father of modern wing-shooting. Probably no less wonderful shot than he could have had influence enough to have changed a style of shotgun aiming that was once universal.

The " one eye " method of sighting a shotgun is not altogether obsolete yet. Many a veteran sportsman has shot long and successfully in this way and will not change; neither is there good reason why he should, for it is hard to teach an old dog new tricks, nor does he learn them quite so well as he knew the old. Nevertheless it is true that few or no expert shots ever close an eye in aiming to-day, though some of them in effect *sight* exactly the same as though they did. The writer has followed the Carver scheme of *gun pointing* more years than he can remember, and among all his friends who shoot well, especially in the uplands, there are none who have any other method of aiming.

Many who point a gun without regard to sight or rib do it unconsciously. As an example a shooting companion of mine who found difficulty in connecting with crossing birds concluded that a patent sight with three beads would assist him greatly. With a bird passing to the left he would use the right bead, and he figured to a mathematical nicety just how far ahead that would throw his charge. After a shot of the kind that usually troubled him, which he missed exactly as before, I asked him where he had held that off bead. He admitted blankly that he never had seen it, and neither could he remember ever seeing one of those three beads afterward when making a quick shot though they were big enough to cover a balloon. He soon threw the patent sight aside as being theoretically fine but practically worthless.

ONE EYE SIGHTING

One eye sighting is distinctly slow and is not adapted to killing game that in the nature of its flight is either imperfectly outlined or rapidly gets beyond range. One eye aiming implies that the instant the gun comes to the shoulder there shall be a pause in its movement while the eye adjusts itself to the sight, or, as it is called, finds it. This focusing the eye upon the sight necessarily dims the vision of the target, for there is no such thing as the human eye focusing perfectly both upon the gun sight and the game. Notwithstanding this the target can be seen, even though it appear shadowy, and the sight placed upon it very accurately; indeed, if the game were not moving, or the shot was directed straight at it, it could be placed with greater precision than in any other way. But it occurs not infrequently that after you have paused to find the sight, the opportunity is gone, either the game cannot be seen again or not quickly enough to cover it before it escapes.

Further, the principle involved in the one eye use of gunsights is that if they do not align perfectly with the target on the first attempt, withhold your fire and never pull trigger until *sure* of your aim. Naturally this theory of obtaining

"AIMING" THE GUN

a second and surer sight when needful is rarely put in practice in wing-shooting, and if it were the result would be a pottering inefficiency that would last through life. The gun-pointing shot doesn't do things that way, since nothing short of a house intervening would prevent his shooting exactly on time.

Finding the sights, whether with one or both eyes open, and putting the focused bead upon the target is beyond question the most accurate way of aiming a gun, as witness that it has been adopted by all riflemen who are obliged to do fine holding. The very finest sighting that I have ever seen done was accomplished with a telescope having a big leather blinder attached to the rear which entirely covered the left eye, thus permitting it to remain wide open without seeing anything. Using a sight of this kind shots can be called within one inch at two hundred yards. This means that at shotgun range of forty yards, a sighting error of one-fifth of an inch could be detected; the absurdity of such close sighting can be noted by recalling that a shotgun pattern covers at least thirty inches at the distance.

What is required in wing-shooting is no such hair-splitting aim, but that we cover the target with the utmost dispatch and pull on the instant —not a hundredth of a second sooner or later.

Indeed pulling a hundredth of a second too soon or the hundredth of a second too late will make more difference as to where our shot charge lands than any variation that can occur with the finest sight or no sight at all.

While I am opposed on principle to the novice learning to sight a shotgun with one eye shut or both eyes open, in fact to *sighting* the arm at all, believing that so taught he can never become a first rate performer on all sorts of game, yet I have seen so much excellent work in wildfowl shooting by men who closed one eye or who focused on the sight that I hesitate to say it is not an effective style of firing at ducks or any bird of large size that is habitually outlined against the sky. In shooting of this kind the game is often seen while approaching and allowance can be made for the time required to focus on the sights; neither is it requisite that the gun be handled with such rapidity as in ordinary upland work.

Success with wildfowl is more due to correct estimates of distance and speed of flight than to manner of aiming, and since there is never any question of being able to see the bird, even with half an eye, it is probable that any system of sighting or pointing the gun can be made about equally effective.

BINOCULAR SHOOTING—TWO-EYE AIMING

Two-eye aiming, or binocular shooting, has all the advantages of closing one eye even for rifle firing while a distinctly clearer view of the target is obtained and distances can be estimated more positively. All of us who were taught to close one eye can well remember that the instant we blinded the left eye to find the sight, the bird at once appeared to be a great deal farther away. I can recall that more than once when a boy I had shut the left eye and then decided that the quail was out of range, after which I opened both eyes and found it still well within reach.

It is no doubt true that with only one eye a gunner could finally learn to judge distances as well as though he had the use of both, but when from birth to age he uses both eyes to see and estimate distances a million times to where he does once with an eye shut, it reasonably follows that he will do better work in the style in which he has been trained, even though that training were not with a gun. Therefore we can take it as a simple statement of fact that with both eyes open we can the most accurately estimate the distance that game is from us, the speed of its flight, and the lead necessary in order to kill. Moreover we can secure equally fine sight with both eyes open, either with shotgun or rifle, provided one eye alone governs the line of sight or is focused upon the sights. This eye is then said to be the master eye for the reason that the brain

Gun-Pointing—With Both Eyes Open

pays attention only to what this eye is doing. The other eye sees just the same, but of its vision the brain fails to keep any record.

Ordinarily it is supposed that the master eye

has the stronger vision, which entitles it to govern, but this does not follow by any means. In shooting from the right shoulder the right eye controls, not because its strength is greater, but for the simple reason that the brain has been *trained* to register only what this eye sees. It may be the stronger eye or it may not, nor would this make much difference unless its vision were extremely defective while that of the other was normal. Ninety-nine times in a hundred one eye governs the line of sight entirely because it has been trained to do this and for no other reason.

The usual manner of testing the eyes for shooting is to hold up an object a proper distance from them and align it with a point beyond while keeping both eyes open. Now close the left eye and if the alignment doesn't change, the right eye governs, but if on shutting the left eye the line of aim swings to the left the wrong optic has been in control, and the student will have to begin training the right eye to assume the mastery or learn to shoot from the left shoulder. Either can be done, but it is much simpler and easier as a rule to put the brain to making its records from the proper eye. It might be noted, in passing, that in case of an experienced shot no eye tests are necessary, for the one with which he has been accustomed to sighting is certain to govern.

The style of aiming with both eyes open may be exactly the same as with one closed; that is, the gun is brought up and there is a slight pause long enough for the eye to find the front sight which is then placed upon the point of aim. The focusing of the eye upon the front sight, however, will probably not be so sharp as with the left eye shut, with the consequence that the vision of the game will be less dimmed. The man accustomed to aiming with one eye closed may find it best to teach himself to shoot with both eyes open while still focusing upon the sight after his acquired fashion. However, this is not the favorite or most effective mode of two-eye aiming. Modern wing shots have pronounced in favor of the

CARVER METHOD OF GUN POINTING

While this style of shotgun aiming is of modern origin, in fact originated with Doctor Carver, yet it is the oldest of all systems of directing a missile. It was used by the rock slingers, the spear throwers, the dart casters, and was brought to the greatest perfection by the long-bowmen. Shooting in this fashion an Indian will drive a penny from between a split stick with half his shots at fifty feet, or strike a running deer at three hundred, and doubtless the Anglo-Saxon bowmen were much better shots than any Indian.

Gun pointing was the recognized manner of aiming of all our western "bad men" and gun fighters whose gun play was entirely too rapid to be directed by any description of gun sights. In combined quickness and accuracy, from foot or horseback, the work of these men has never been equaled, but their system of shooting is now becoming a lost art because it was not found the best adapted to target practice. Perhaps in course of time gun pointing will hold sway in short range shooting with every variety of firearm, for the military tendency at present is to encourage rapidity of fire.

Probably it was from the western gun-fighter that Doctor Carver, a western man, got his idea of the correct way of sighting a shotgun. If the man with the six-shooter could hit nickels thrown into the air, rabbits running, a man on a galloping horse while himself mounted, or swing his weapon on a foe with such rapidity that the eye could not follow the movements, then why couldn't a man with a shotgun place its thirty inch pattern upon a flying bird without glueing his eye to any sights? Carver believed that it could be done, and he showed the skeptical until everybody was ready to go away and do likewise.

Gun pointing has been miscalled instinctive aiming, though in reality there is nothing instinctive about it. There can be nothing instinctive in doing a thing that we have learned to accomplish through repeating a performance thousands of times. It is merely perfecting an art that we have been acquiring from babyhood, that of being able to point the finger or something else directly at an object toward which we are looking fixedly. We might as well say that we write instinctively, because we give no thought to what the next stroke will be. In civilized human beings training takes the place of instinct which is a very imperfect factor, though it must be admitted that every man has inherited tendencies.

Shooting a pistol in the old western way consisted simply in extending the hand quickly in the direction of the target and pulling on the instant. This one-hand gun pointing is the most natural method and the easiest to acquire because we have been at it a good many years before we ever gripped a gun. Shooting a shotgun differs from it only in that the *piece is pointed with both hands* in place of one, and while the method is more difficult to acquire it is steadier and more reliable, because with the butt of the weapon at the shoulder and both hands holding it we have a firmer control than if the piece were directed entirely with the one hand. Shooting a shotgun in the Carver fashion, in its primary principle, is merely training the two hands to point at the exact spot at which the eyes are looking or the brain directs, without any lost motion or focus upon sights.

Shooting a revolver in the western manner, with movement of hand too fast for the eye to follow, is in reality juggling a pistol, and muscles and nerves must undergo the same training as those of a juggler who keeps half a dozen balls in the air with one hand. The wing-shot who aims by pointing also juggles his weapon in a way, though the training necessary to do this is not so severe because the movements are not especially rapid. Nevertheless he undergoes a degree of training that insures his weapon being aligned automatically or without conscious effort before he becomes an expert shot. When he has reached a stage where none of the movements of his piece require conscious supervision, then they are said to be instinctive, though, as we have seen, instinct has nothing whatever to do with it; it is training pure and simple.

The advantages of pointing a shotgun in place of getting the eye close down to the barrels and aligning rib and sight are these: Point your finger at an object quickly, without any effort to sight or closing an eye, and you will find that while it is directed precisely, yet nevertheless you are glancing some distance above the finger. Now close one eye and you will note at once a tendency to drop the head and *sight* the finger. The same optical principle applies to pointing and sighting a gun; under the former system you naturally keep the barrels well down out of the line of vision, but at the same time direct them at an object with exactly the same precision as in the other way.

Moreover in pointing a gun by means of a thorough training of the hands, you are in a measure independent of fit of gunstock. Indeed, in my own experience and that of others, any gun can be shot accurately so long as the drop of stock is not so great as to bring the barrels within the line of sight, or where they will interfere with a clear view of the target. Correct alignment is not nearly so dependent upon drop of stock as it is upon the position of the two hands grasping grip and fore-end.

For instance, if you are accustomed to a gun that is grasped nearly in the line of fire, and you then attempt to shoot with one having a deep fore-end which places the left hand low, or a piece with grip set low behind the frame, you will at once note a feeling of uncertainty as to where you are pointing. I should therefore conclude that an accustomed grip and fore-stock were of as much

"AIMING" THE GUN

importance as drop at comb and grip. Additionally it should be noted that if the hands are to do the pointing unassisted by sights, they should grasp the piece well apart, that is with the left hand extended as far as possible without strain, and the places where they grip the arm should never vary an iota.

Given a gun that I have grown to with use, I find that I can shoot as effectively when holding my face several inches from the gunstock, really not inclining the head toward the stock in the least, but holding it perfectly erect, some inches above the line of the barrels and well to one side. I have further dropped my head toward the left shoulder in place of the right and struck my bird with the same facility, proving that the hands were accomplishing their work automatically without regard to the position of the sighting eye with reference to the line of sight. Dropping the stock low on the shoulder, or jamming the comb tight against the cheek made not a particle of difference so long as the automatic action of the hands was not interfered with by trying to govern them directly by means of the sight.

In gun pointing the sight should never be seen, nor rib, nor barrel, neither should they be even thought of, for if the eye is permitted to interfere with the calculations of the brain, two bosses of equal authority are installed, with the obvious result that nothing will be accomplished. In this style of aiming the gun should be swung methodically, with mechanical uniformity of movement, and the trigger pressed the moment you *feel* that the aim is correct. No mystery need be made of this feeling of being right, for it is merely the signal of the brain to the nerves that the work has been well accomplished. The same feeling is in evidence when a baseball pitcher has released a ball which he *knows* will split the pan, or when the billiardist or golf player has made a true stroke.

In gun pointing long and short barrels can be shot with much less variation in the holding than when the eye governs the line of sight, for with the latter method a long sighting plane is a positive advantage. The hands will do their work with the same facility be the barrels long or short, since these are never seen, but length of tubes is to be preferred for other than sighting reasons, as balance of the arm, steadiness in swinging to a given point, reduced recoil, etc.

Relative to the rapidity of shooting under the two systems, when a rifle is fired the two sights are first placed exactly in a line which is then directed to the point of aim. Should this line of sight not cover the target precisely the piece is not discharged but the sights are swung on again and again before the trigger is pulled; it may take the rifleman from fifteen to sixty seconds to secure a satisfactory aim and pull. This sort of aiming is absolutely impracticable in shotgun shooting for obvious reasons, in fifteen seconds the target might be two or three hundred yards away.

In some descriptions of wing-shooting, as quail or ruffed grouse in the woods, the gun is discharged within three-quarters of a second after the brain has realized that the bird is on the wing; during this length of time the shooter takes position, brings his gun to his shoulder, selects the point of aim, directs his piece there, and presses the trigger. No " second sight " can be obtained under such circumstances, whatever error the eye may detect at the instant of firing, and accuracy is absolutely dependent upon the mechanical training of the hands which direct the gun. By putting the eye and mind upon the gun-sights these can be noted very clearly, but while doing this *the bird is lost*.

The one advantage in " sighting," among all its disadvantages, is that the novice can more readily detect errors in holding. He cannot prevent the shot he is firing from going wrong, but he may be able to analyze every movement of his piece and so discover which particular feature needs correction; he might be making some mistake with mechanical regularity and certainty, just as in writing he may produce some ill formed letter and be quite unable to alter its form except with deliberate care. Perhaps it is true that a high degree of skill in gun pointing is the result of a post-graduate course in wing-shooting rather than the A.B.C. of the art.

Now there may be doubt in the mind of the beginner or others as to whether a shotgun can be pointed accurately enough invariably to place the pattern upon the target, for it is not claimed that sufficient precision can be developed for deliberate rifle shooting. With a view to settling this question the writer made a series of experiments at twenty yards with a 22 rifle from which the sights had been removed.

With a well balanced rifle, handling like a shotgun, balls after ball could be placed in a six-inch circle, the majority of them going into a four inch. No attempt was made to level or even see the barrel and the arm was fired with the same rapidity as a shotgun at quail.

In order to be sure that the barrel was not being leveled or sighted a blinder was built up on the barrel over the position of the ordinary rear sight; any attempt to sight over this would have thrown the bullets two feet high. After a few shots the results were just the same as before, and so long as the target could be seen the gun could be pointed there with ample accuracy to kill every bird with a shotgun. Diagrams are here presented of ten-shot targets made in this fashion, both with the naked barrel and the blinder at-

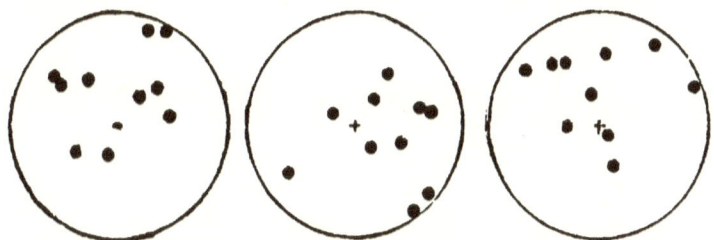

THREE TEN-SHOT TARGETS MADE WITH A .22 RIFLE AT 20 YARDS WITH A BLINDER OVER THE REAR SIGHT, SHOWING THE EFFECT OF BINOCULAR GUN POINTING

tached. Of course such shooting is dependent somewhat upon the skill of the marksman, but so is any other kind of shooting for the matter of that.

In some measure every man must be a law unto himself in his work with a gun. While I use the pointing system of aiming for all game, yet some of my shooting acquaintances tell me that whereas they can point very accurately at anything flying near the ground, at birds passing overhead they have a feeling of uncertainty as to where they are holding that leads them to prefer aligning the barrels by direct sight of eye in such work. Doubtless it is all much a matter of training and habit.

CHAPTER III

SNAP-SHOOTING, DELIBERATE SWING, AND RAPID SWING

ALMOST every writer on the topic of field shooting will at some time mention making a snap shot at a bird, or perhaps covering another and then swinging ahead before firing. The reader can readily gather from these essays that snapping is a very prompt way of delivering a shot, while the swing is both more deliberate and more accurate. It is not likely, however, that, taught by books solely, the student will ever be able to fix in his own mind exactly what a snap shot is nor what constitutes a swinging shot, further than that one is discharged in much the shorter time. Still less will he have grounds for deciding which particular style of shooting he ought himself to adopt.

The object of this chapter is to analyze these systems of aiming, making as plain as possible what constitutes a snap shot, what a deliberate swing, and the difference in principle between a deliberate and a rapid swing. Simple diagrams

42   WING AND TRAP-SHOOTING

and drawings are used to illustrate with the hope of making the subject plainer to the beginner in wing-shooting.

The term "line of swing" will be used frequently in this chapter so it is well to give an early explanation of its meaning. The accom-

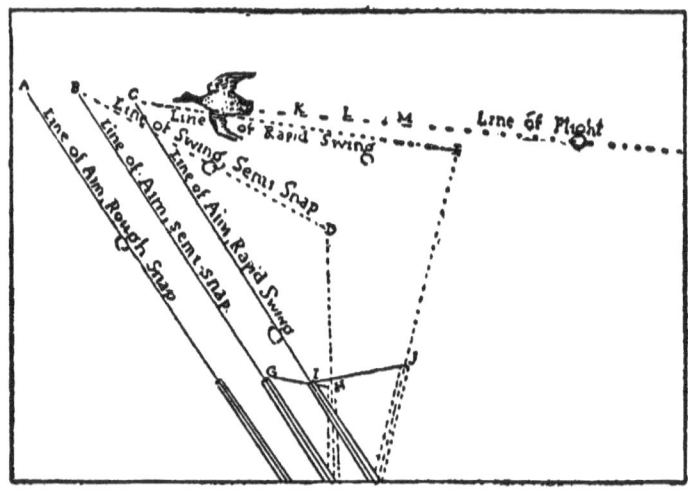

ROUGH SNAP, SEMI-SNAP, AND RAPID SWING

panying diagram shows the line of swing. It is the line covered by the moving gunsights from the time the piece strikes the shoulder or the sights are caught to where they are pointed when the gun is fired. The character of this gun movement or sight movement constitutes the difference in the three styles of gun aiming.

Technically, snap shooting has no line of swing, the aim being taken before the gun is brought up, the sights are thrown directly to the desired point and the arm is discharged the instant the butt hits the shoulder. While this is snap shooting proper, it is a very ineffective manner of firing even at an object at rest, for the reason that when the butt jams into the shoulder muscles the latter give and then rebound, causing the gun muzzle to vibrate to such an extent as to insure a miss except with a very wide spread of pattern. Selecting a point of aim before the gun is thrown to the shoulder is making a pretty fine calculation too, it must be admitted; the bird might spring to the north of you, and without a moment's hesitation you would have to know the precise spot to the northwest where the shot charge would meet it.

Such absolute judgment of speed and angle of flight is next to impossible, and the experienced gunner never attempts snap shooting in this fashion, except when he perceives that the opportunity to shoot at all will be so fleeting that it is either a rough snap shot or none. Impressed with the belief that wing-shooting is merely jerking up the gun and lamming away, the novice is liable to practice just this sort of snapping, with the result that when he does hit he cannot tell why, nor give a reason for his misses. The expert who can handle his gun like a part of himself cannot shoot successfully in this manner, much less a tyro.

There is another style of snap shooting, however, that is widely practiced by nearly all clever upland shots. It consists of throwing the gun close to the game with the motion of bringing it to the shoulder, but always sufficiently under it. From this point beneath the target the line of sight travels in a direct line with great quickness to the point of aim where the gun is discharged.

Suppose a grouse has sprung from the brush and is circling to the left and rising. It has been estimated that a grouse or a quail will be ten feet into the air before a man's mind can give his nerves and muscles any instruction whatever. Then if a rough snap shot were to be made the gun would be at once slung ahead of the bird and there fired. The difficulty of making such a shot is obvious. In the first place the motion of raising a gun to the shoulder is complicated compared with moving to a given spot after it is up and steady. Moreover in a rough snap there is never any change of aim from the spot the mind estimates as right. The gun is simply thrown to that place and fired.

Orders have been given which the mind cannot alter if it would, and even should the bird be killed

SNAP-SHOOTING 45

meantime by another gunner the snapped piece would inevitably be discharged precisely the same at that square. Thus we see that the problems confronting the rough snap shot are: a mechanical inability to jam a gun to the shoulder and shoot to a given spot and the extraordinary judgment required to foretell where the bird will be when the arm is ready to fire.

We have all heard of some snap shots that were as quick as lightning, and of course if this were literally so the shot could be sent to the first possible place, but it should be remembered that the man is probably walking with his gun down, and during the short space of say half a second he must get his feet into position, make his estimates, and bring up his gun—meantime the bird will be doing something you may be sure, covering not less than twenty-five feet. Nevertheless it is not to be doubted that the quicker the shooter, the lighter his gun, and the more open his pattern, the simpler his problem becomes.

At best, however, shooting in this fashion, an expert could not expect to connect with more than one bird in three. Knowing this the skilled wing-shot would never attempt the rough snap except that suppose at the natural place of aim there was a tree with brush beyond. Reaching this tree, the grouse would be safe so nothing remains but to chance the lightning snap. It follows that the novice should never deliver a rough snap unless any other kind of an aim is impossible either because the bird will be out of sight or possibly out of range; in either of which events it is to be preferred to not shooting at all.

The second or practical style of snap shooting is much more reliable. With this method the gun is thrown up below the target, first, that the view of the game may not be obscured in the least; second, that time may be given to the gun muzzle to cease its vibrations ere it covers the point of aim; third, that while the line of sight is moving steadily yet rapidly to the point where the charge is to go the trigger finger can be given due warning to pull; fourth, the estimates for lead and speed of flight are greatly simplified because only taken from the time the gun is up and not from the rising of the bird. The problem here is to make the line of swing cross the line of flight of the bird, and this is comparatively easy.

In its principle rough snap shooting is to throw the gun to the point of aim without a line of swing. That of semi-snap shooting is to *intersect* the line of flight with the line of swing in the shortest and most direct way. For instance with some angles of flight the gun might be thrown too far ahead and then the " line of aim " would be carried back toward the flying target. Naturally this happens seldom unless the bird changes his course, the skilled shot endeavoring to throw up his weapon in such a position that it will only be necessary to lift it straight to the spot where it will be fired.

The more accurate the judgment of the sportsman as to the bird's speed of flight, the nearer he will come to throwing his piece to the proper place with a consequent shorter line of swing and a quicker shot. But in doing this it should not be forgotten that the line of aim must always be of sufficient length to steady the gun before it covers the mark and to fairly warn the pulling finger. Otherwise you are on the bird, as they say, before you know it, and the result is an almost inevitable miss. This not infrequently happens with straightaway birds, where in the nature of things the swing is short and is a most productive and irritating source of misses. Indeed, it is an axiom with veteran field shots that the driving bird requires the steadiest of all holding.

Successful snap shooting necessitates a very quick and sensitive trigger. Bear in mind that the line of swing merely intercepts the line of flight and can only do so at one point, at one instant; any dwelling upon the trigger, a pressure that comes the smallest fraction of a second too soon or too late, leads to certain missing. The bird may be traveling fifty feet a second, the line of swing a hundred feet a second or more; should the trigger yield the hundredth of a second fast or slow the game will be missed a foot. Any irregularity of trigger pulling is fatal, and a man who needs a greater time than a fiftieth of a second to release his trigger had better adopt some other style of aiming.

Snap shooting or semi-snap shooting is an effective style of aiming only upon birds that are not changing their angle with regard to the gun too rapidly—that is upon straightaway or quartering birds. Should the quarry rise and swing about the gun would inevitably have to follow it if the piece came up promptly, or a swift flying fowl might come in from the right and pass to the left before it could be covered, with the result that the gun would have to swing after and overtake it before being discharged. This would lead to the third mode of aiming, technically known as a rapid swing.

In this style the line of swing either travels directly along the line of flight or preferably takes a parallel course just beneath it for the sake of an unobstructed view. The working principle of the rapid swing is that the gun is invariably

SNAP-SHOOTING

aligned behind the bird and the "line of aim" is then swung after it much faster than the bird is moving, until it overtakes and passes the moving mark to the point where the charge is sent to catch the bird.

The strength of this system of gun aiming lies in this: The gun moving in the path of flight of the game takes the elevation automatically. In ilustration of this, should the bird be rising the line of swing rises also and will continue to do so after passing the bird, necessarily striking its mark unless the course of the target alters radically. Of course an identical rule would apply were the bird descending, climbing, or taking any other angle of elevation so long as the line of swing followed the line of flight and passed it the proper distance.

Rapid swing simplifies lead also, for should the line of swing be traveling three times as fast as the bird flies an estimated lead of one foot would place the charge three feet ahead of the bird, the gain being made during the interim of pressing the trigger and the passage of the shot up the barrel. Moreover it must be borne in mind that now the line of aim is not intersecting that of flight but traveling with it, which permits considerable latitude in trigger pulling. Should the gunner be a trifle quick or slow the charge, still

50   *WING AND TRAP-SHOOTING*

being in line, will probably catch the mark with some portion of the pattern.

Almost every skillful wildfowl gunner uses the rapid swing, and many do so in the uplands as

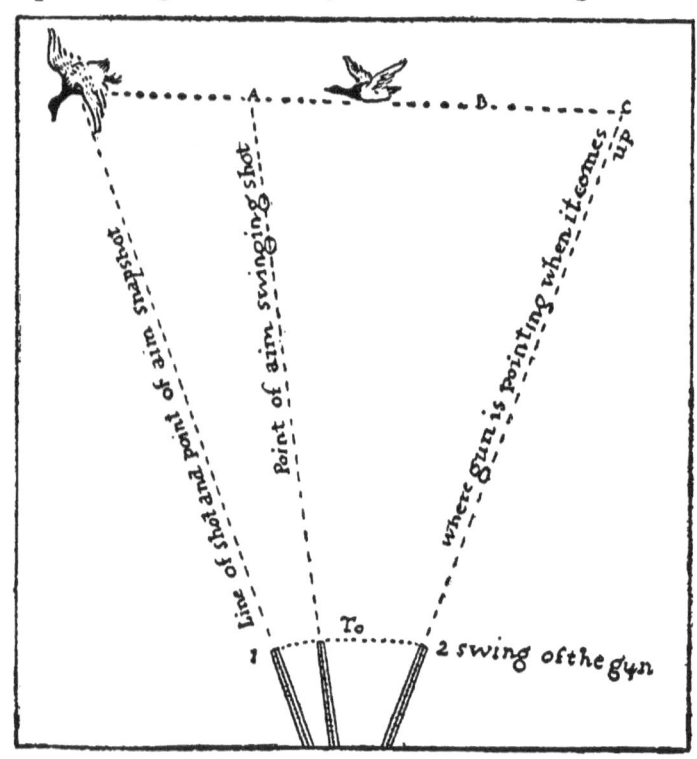

The Difference in Lead Between a Snap Shot and a Swinging Shot

well. Birds with a speed of from sixty to one hundred miles an hour are entirely too fast to be snapped with any certainty.

The diagram indicates the difference in lead

SNAP-SHOOTING

between a swinging shot and a snap shot. The bird is supposed to be distant from the gun one hundred feet, and is traveling at the rate of one hundred feet a second. The normal velocity of a shot charge over a one hundred foot course is eight hundred feet a second, and at this velocity it would require one-eighth of a second for the pellets to reach the mark. In one-eighth of a second the fowl would fly twelve and a half feet which is the theoretical lead necessary for shot and target to connect. If the line of aim intersects the line of flight at right angles—as in snap shooting—the full theoretical lead must be taken, and if there is any dwelling upon the trigger a further allowance must be given.

But with a swinging shot in which the line of aim travels three times as fast as the bird, this sighting line will move six feet in the fiftieth of a second required for a quick man to pull the trigger and for the passage of the shot up the barrel. Hence we have lead for a snap shot twelve and a half feet, lead for a swinging shot six and a half feet. In case of the man who requires the maximum length of time to pull, or 6-100 of a second, a further lead of six feet would have to be given with a snap shot, or a total of eighteen and a half feet. No man could make such an estimate.

By consulting experienced wing-shots it will

be learned that hardly any two of them will make the same estimate for the lead necessary to kill at a given distance; neither theoretically nor practically are they holding at the same place. In fact with the rapid swing every man is a law unto himself, the distance he holds ahead being governed by the rapidity of his swing, his time in trigger pulling, and his habit of maintaining a uniform gun movement after pressing the trigger. One shooter might swing rapidly but would check his piece at the moment of firing and so lose all the advantage of swinging; another would accelerate the motion of his muzzle at the instant of firing and so gain more than six feet. The same thing could be done by the individual of slow trigger, who if he pulled in 6-100 of a second could actually gain eighteen feet and would not need to make any lead at all—neither would he hit anything, for it might well be stated now that a pull of as slow as six one-hundredths of a second is quite too slow for wing-shooting.

Nevertheless some of the best duck shots that I have ever known stated positively that they made no allowance whatever for speed of flight or distance of the mark further than to merely hold in front and swing. Watching them at work, I arrived at the conclusion that they made the necessary gain entirely by the rapidity with which they swung—for all of them moved their pieces very swiftly—and not by any hesitation on the trigger.

Doubtless the acme of wing-shooting is to be able to swing with such rapidity and uniformity as to obviate the necessity for any lead, but it will not do for the novice to attempt to graduate his first year in school. Indeed, the average sportsman never learns to shoot in this way, neither should he endeavor to do so unless so situated that he can fire shot after shot, days, weeks, and months in succession.

Indeed the swifter the swing the graver the problem of so governing it that the shot can be placed with sufficient precision to strike the mark. The neophyte can readily learn this for himself by attempting to shoot at a stationary mark while swinging the gunsights past it. Experience soon teaches the gunner about how fast he can swing successfully, and his endeavor henceforth should be to make this swing as mechanically uniform as possible, studying carefully the results which he secures from it.

A semi-snap shot and a rapid swing may readily merge into one another. The gunner may throw up his weapon with a view to making a snap shot, but finding the bird has passed his gun, he must needs swing after it. In the same way when intending to place his piece upon the line of the bird's flight he might fall below it, being then obliged to both swing with the bird and to raise his gun to intersect its flight.

The two styles of aiming are readily used in conjunction, also, as in live pigeon shooting where the shooter ordinarily makes a practical snap with the first barrel and a rapid swing with the second. A like system is preferred by the crack field shot who snaps with his first barrel before the game is at top speed and then swings on with the second should he miss. One thing must forever be borne in mind by the swinging shot and that is never to check the gun when pulling the trigger.

In upland shooting upon such game as quail, snipe, chickens, partridge, and woodcock, birds that rise near the gun, nearly every shot can be taken without any allowance for lead or elevation, it being necessary merely to swing upon the line of flight past the game and fire with the result of killing nine birds out of ten, which is a pretty good percentage in any event. The truth is that in such work, especially in the brush, there is no time to think of allowance for lead, but this can always be secured automatically by swinging, and therein is the advantage over any description of snap shot.

There remains to be described the deliberate

SNAP-SHOOTING

swing. It fits in with the old one-eye manner of aiming and is becoming antiquated along with it. With the deliberate swing the game is first covered usually by throwing the line of sight in front of it, and then moving with the target, at the proper distance in advance until the trigger is pulled. The principle involved is to maintain the requisite lead while the trigger is being pressed, continuing the swing at the same rate until the charge is out of the gun. In theory this system of aiming is the most accurate of all, because whether the trigger is pressed instantly or dwelt upon the pattern will with like certainty reach the desired lead. For instance, if the line of aim is traveling three feet in advance of the line of flight, which distance is maintained until the shot are on the way, it cannot matter whether the trigger is pressed in 1-100 of a second or 6-100.

Obviously with this system of aiming no gain is made by the swing and the same allowance for speed and distance is required as though the target was snapped.

The trouble with this mode of aiming is that it develops a very slow, poky, pottering style. There being no precise moment when the trigger *must* be pulled, the gunner almost invariably acquires the ill habit of dwelling upon the trigger. For this reason the deliberate swing cannot be used upon any game that is quick in its movements, that swerves and dodges like a snipe or a quail. Hence such a slow system of aiming is not adapted to anything except waterfowl or such birds as are seen approaching and remain within gun shot some time.

I have seen most excellent work upon wildfowl by those who swung deliberately in front of the target and am ready to believe that the style can be made very effective upon such birds. In duck shooting where the birds are passing and have acquired maximum speed it certainly has the advantage of any sort of snap work.

Nevertheless my advice to the beginner would be to acquire the rapid swing. It accomplishes everything that can be done with the deliberate and does it quicker and better, with a minimum of nerve expenditure. It requires double the expenditure of nerve force to shoot deliberately that it does to pull quickly, and no man should endeavor to develop the slow style unless nature has made him steady and phlegmatic.

CHAPTER IV

PRIMARY LESSONS

ALMOST every boy with an inborn taste for shooting will have learned to aim a gun and pull trigger before he becomes old enough to tramp widely afield or handle a fowling piece. Emphatically is this true of the youth so fortunate as to be born in the country. However, there may be youngsters with the ill luck to be crowded by houses and people all their lives, with whom the longing to hunt and shoot must be deferred to more mature years. The city boy whose instincts waiting on opportunity, must needs survive all urban temptations, makes the most determined and enthusiastic of sportsmen when finally stock and shoulder fit together. Hungry for the fields and the whistle of birds' wings, he never gets enough from twenty years to his three score and ten. With a view to assisting him as much as I may in his first lessons this chapter is written.

An old disused barn in the country is a great

place for preliminary practice with a shotgun. Secure some large sheets of paper, blacken the center, and tack them up on the barn. Shoot at twenty yards because at that distance the pattern will not spread too much to easily observe its effect. Select very lightly loaded shells for this kind of work, two and a half drams of powder are enough and lighter loads are better if they can be procured. Recoil always appears more severe when the target is stationary, and it takes practice so to hold the weapon that the arms and hands absorb most of the jar. The object now is to acquire confidence in yourself and the gun, carefully guarding against a tendency to flinch which is liable to develop into a most annoying habit, nearly fatal to good wing shooting.

A few shots should enable the learner to place his pattern regularly upon the center of the target. When this can be done with a deliberate aim begin snapping. Throw the gun quickly to the shoulder, pointed at the target, and without checking the motion raise it to the center and fire as you come up. If the trigger fails to yield at the exact time, take the piece down, throw it up and try again. What you are striving for in this is a correct trigger pull, the lock working precisely on time, without any checking

PRIMARY LESSONS

the gun for a second sight or any attempt to hold it still upon the target.

An axiom of shotgun shooting is that the aim is never to be held still upon anything—in this differing radically from the rifle. The trigger should be pressed, therefore, without checking the regular rising movement of the barrels, the pulling and upward movement of the sight being so well timed that the discharge will take place just before the center is covered.

Press the trigger, not by any conscious crooking of the forefinger, but by tightening the grip of both hands, the one pushing forward and the other drawing back. This is not only the right manner of pulling trigger on a shotgun, but tightening the grip of the hands enables the gunner to catch the recoil just as the blow of a fist is warded off before it gathers momentum.

Having learned to strike the mark with a straight upward snap, as directed, now begin swinging on from side to side, first from the right and then from the left. Swing evenly past the target and pull as the line of sight goes by, being careful not to check up at the moment of firing. Probably this shooting with a right and left swing needs practice to obtain the desired accuracy, but keep at it until the charge regularly reaches its mark. Swing slowly at first, but later increase the speed until the center can be struck with the piece swinging smartly. Doubtless with a rapid swing a tendency will be noted for the charge to pass the center on the line of aim, but that can be avoided by pulling quicker, which is one of the things to be learned.

With proficiency, vary the line of swing with every shot, sometimes coming on from the right, again from the left, then straight up and quartering. These lessons are the foundation of wing shooting, so take plenty of time with them and do not expect to accomplish everything in one day. Twenty-five shots are enough for one practice, since among other things you must develop nerve force rather than expend it to the point of exhaustion. Remember that half the people who go afield never learn to shoot, and a large share of the others spend the remainder of their shooting days trying to eradicate the bad habits acquired in early youth.

Having learned to strike your target with a gun moving fast or slow, with the line of sight swinging in every direction except down, you now have command of the gun and can take up the second problem, exchanging the stationary for a flying target. Here is where shooting schools are an advantage since they have a movable target which travels across the barn at any

PRIMARY LESSONS 61

desired angle, with a rate of speed that can be regulated from very slow to as fast as a bird flies. The benefit of a flying target with a background that would instantly show the impact of the pattern is not to be doubted, faults of holding being detected at once. However, shooting schools are not a very common institution in this country, though in their place we have the clay bird trap and artificial targets.

If you have access to the grounds of a trap shooting club, go there for practice. If possible enlist the services of some more experienced friend who can point out your errors and instruct you as to where to hold. Stand as close to the trap as you like and take only easy, straightaway, low flying birds in the beginning, later changing to quartering targets. Becoming skilled enough to hit these, go out into the field and have the birds thrown past you at different distances to one side and the other.

Endeavor to obtain every description of shot that is likely to be afforded by field shooting. Have the birds thrown while walking up on the trap with gun down in its ordinary carrying position, and instruct the trapper to start his bird at unexpected times, even when your back is turned when he should of course warn you as the target starts. A like method should be followed when the gun is out in the field. Naturally the nearer conditions can be made to approach field shooting the more valuable the practice. Getting behind the traps, with gun to shoulder, and shooting at birds always at the same angle of flight teaches very little except mechanical regularity of performance which can be acquired at the barn. But rightly used artificial targets can be made a very beneficial experience.

The English method is to mount the traps in a tower from which the birds are thrown over the shooter's head and past him. Such practice would prove very helpful to the inexperienced duck shot, as it is with the British driven game. Unfortunately our gun clubs never mount their traps in a tower or endeavor to teach anything except the making of big scores. For this reason a man may become an expert at the traps and yet possess but a trifling amount of skill in the field.

The writer, a country boy, with no clay targets to shoot at, got his first lessons in pass shooting by means of an arrow-shaped piece of wood known as a dart. The dart is driven by means of a short stick, similar to the rod of a fly fisherman, though not so long and limber. This rod has a short, strong line with a knot in the end which engages with a notch cut into the dart about one-third of the way from the point, the dart being cast by means of an overhead swing the same as in throwing a fly. Our dart can be made of light, cheap wood, from three to five feet long, with a large, flat head and a broad shank. It can be sent a distance of one hundred and fifty yards, with a velocity in the beginning of its flight higher than that attained by any bird.

The object is to strike the broad head of the dart and if the charge falls back anywhere else along its length the novice knows that he has not made sufficient allowance for speed and distance. When thrown rapidly the flight of this projectile is practically level, neither does it lose velocity as quickly as an artificial clay bird. The dart can be thrown at any desired angle except straight away from the gun. Practice at the dart is especially good training for flight shooting at wildfowl, and the boy who has become expert in striking the head of a shaft traveling a hundred and fifty feet a second will have little trouble in connecting with ducks or any bird of similar flight. Of course a good assistant is necessary to this kind of practice, but any athletic boy will enjoy casting the dart as much as the gunner will shooting at it.

Shooting at clay birds as they are commonly

thrown at gun club meets is not without benefit to the upland gunner, but the experience avails the marsh shooter very little: indeed, his acquired habit of holding close to his birds is very hard to overcome even when he has learned where to hold. Not so the man who shoots at a dart which may be traveling two hundred feet a second; he necessarily learns to get out in front—away out.

A hand trap is a convenience where club grounds and traps may not be available. They throw the same clay birds as the ground traps, but are held in the hand which enables the target to be sent in any direction. Good practice can be made by having the assistant throw the bird at unexpected times when both are walking along. The shooter thus learns to be alert, promptly bringing up his gun to take the bird that rises without warning. The trapper may walk behind and send his target past the gun, or even be hidden by hedge and cover, in which case he should call sharply when starting the bird.

Keep up the snapping and swinging practice at the stationary target, at the clay birds, and the dart until expert. It will teach you just as much as getting out into the fields and banging away at non-game birds, which is a very unsportsmanlike thing to do as will be discovered should it ever be attempted in the presence of a veteran bird hunter. Besides shooting song birds is generally forbidden by law.

In all this time do not forget that your endeavor is to make the gun a sort of third arm that will point anywhere you wish as readily as the arm can be thrown in that direction. When no other practice is available, take up the gun in your room or back yard, and placing some empty shells in the chambers, exercise your pointing skill by throwing the piece up quickly, covering some object and pulling the trigger. This is a very valuable drill, alike beneficial to the tyro and the expert. Indeed you can hardly get too much of it, only do not be careless with the work but put heart into it.

We have all laughed about the Englishman who throws up his walking stick to sight every bird that flies past, but really the Briton is right, for there is horse sense in just that kind of practice.

In your target shooting at the barn you may discover that the firing can be accomplished with greater precision by stopping the gun at the exact instant of pressing the trigger, but do not allow that to influence you or change your scheme of pulling trigger with a moving gun. A dangerous habit may become fixed, one that will have to be overcome later when it is found necessary for the arm to keep pace with the swiftest flying game. Furthermore there is the second barrel to be remembered.

The barn is also a convenient background in training to acquire second barrel habits. The right use of the second cartridge is to have it follow the first invariably where the first barrel has crippled or missed, unless two birds have sprung at once and you expect to make a double. When this is the case make no pause to observe the effect of the first shot but continue the swing of the tubes until they cover the second target.

Put up two targets on the barn for second barrel practice, placing them at first on a horizontal line about twenty feet apart. Fire at the right hand target and without stopping the swing cover the second mark and shoot again. You will shortly learn in doing this that some time is required to recover from the recoil of the first shot, and the gun will be thrown out of line. But utilize this time in moving onto the second bullseye which should be sighted as soon as the piece is under control and moving steadily again.

As the practice continues change the position of the targets, sometimes shooting at the right hand first and again at the left; then place one above the other at different angles and various distances apart. Quicken the time as you become expert until not over half a second is re-

PRIMARY LESSONS 67

quired to get onto the second, pull, and shoot. A lightning second barrel shot can swing on with his second barrel and shoot accurately in a quarter of a second, which is the standard of rapidity that the novice should set for himself.

The barn with large sheets of paper will indicate results of this rapid swinging fire more definitely than any live or clay birds, so continue this work until results are perfect, quick time being uniformly maintained with absolute accuracy. Keep the piece swinging after the second shot the same as the first.

After the practice I have described the novice should have little trouble in connecting with a certain number of birds, either in the uplands or marsh, the first time he goes afield. There is no greater difficulty in placing the pattern upon a quail than in striking the clay target, except for the added excitement caused by whirring wings and the anxiety to make a good showing.

Overanxiety to appear well or show shooting skill to your companion is a fruitful source of missing, not only by the beginner, but by the older hand alike. Indeed, if overanxiety and flinching could be eliminated the majority of us would do fifty per cent. better execution. It is well therefore for the student of wing shooting to go afield with a veteran shot in securing his first experience, one that cannot be considered in any sense a rival gunner, but who is anxious to see that his young friend performs well rather than to display his own skill. If such companionship and instruction are unavailable, then go alone and study out the problems in your own way.

Be very careful not to quicken the time you have been acquiring, but rather shoot more deliberately, remembering that any bird you fire at so quickly as not to be able to recall where the gun was held is simply a lost opportunity, no matter whether the bird was killed or missed. The only method of acquiring a solid foundation for future success, is to make your mental calculations quickly and then use your gun to prove your judgment. In plainer phrases do not shoot until you have first decided where to hold, and then put the charge right there with all the skill you possess, making a mental memorandum of every move the bird made, the gun processes necessary to cover him, fire, and the results.

Do not be hurried because your companion is quickest, for every human being learns to walk before he can run. You could not reasonably expect to solve problems in mathematics as readily as a college professor, and take my word for it wing-shooting is no less difficult than mathematics.

PRIMARY LESSONS 69

Do not let misses disturb you, for in the beginning as much can be learned from missing as from hitting, since you have at least been taught where not to hold. The man who cannot learn through his mistakes will never know a great deal, but be sure to analyze errors thoroughly, and know reasons, otherwise experience and practice will leave you about where you started.

It is a fortunate thing for the earnest young sportsman that his mind is impressionable and his memory most tenacious. I can clearly recall the shots that I made twenty-five years ago; just how the bird broke cover, the course of his flight where the gun came to the shoulder, how much it led when the trigger was pulled, the very weed that the bird struck as he fell; even the clumps of feathers, sifting down, are still before me. Opportunity and circumstances being similar, I could repeat the shots in the same old way. None but the young could be impressed so graphically, and no others learn with such ease.

It is not necessary that the student should possess such memory, however, but the moment a shot is fired every detail should be fixed in his mind. The better to do this make a systematic mental diary. Here the bird arose so many paces from the gun, he was at this point when the weapon came up, he bore away from the shooter at an angle of forty-five degrees, slightly rising; the gun came up just so much behind him, and he flew so many yards before being covered and fired upon with a lead of two feet; result, a kill. Try to recall the exact position of the flying target when the mental estimate for lead was made, and if the bird flew farther than you think he should before being shot perhaps the cause can be detected. Remember that a lesson is of no value after it is forgotten and do not forget. The very first thing to be recorded after the mind recovers from the strain of firing is to note where the gun is then pointed. It should swing right along on the path of the bird's flight, and if involuntarily checked at the shot, that is something to be studied and corrected. The average shot never learns to continue his swing upon the line of flight after the bird is dead, but be ambitious to do what the average man cannot accomplish.

At the close of the day's shooting, take your mental diagrams and write them all out on paper. Mark upon the sheet where the bird arose, where you stood, and every evolution of target and gun as previously directed. Study these diagrams and fix in your own mind why you killed and why you missed. If the shot was a scratch or accidental write that down, for many such shots are made in the course of a season, and these daily diagrams are intended for future study.

If you failed to hit give that drawing especial attention, marking the place where you should have held. When at a loss as to where the shot should have been directed, probably your shooting friend can set you right. Above all do not again hold for the exact spot that previously resulted in a failure, unless you can prove to your own satisfaction that the miss resulted from other causes than faulty lead.

If the gunner cannot recall his point of aim at the instant of firing that is something for grave study. It may be that his line of aim is swinging so fast that it is impossible to govern it; he really cannot tell where he is aiming at any precise moment from the time the weapon comes to the shoulder until it is discharged. Again perhaps it is a case of unconscious flinching, and this is always to be suspected where the shooter cannot *see* where his shot has gone.

Bear in mind that flinching is not necessarily the result of batting the eyes but may be simply a cessation of the action of the brain in anticipation of a shock. As a test of flinching shoot more deliberately, which will usually betray the fault by causing the muzzle to waver before the discharge takes place.

I can only repeat again, use the utmost care not to make the same mistake in a like way. Study and analyze, and your hits will soon teach you to kill, while your misses will tell you how not to miss again. When desirous of showing well, learn to select the bird that you know how to kill, the one that is easy for you, be it straight away, left quartered, or what not. But if simply desirous of improving your shooting, let the easy birds go and choose only the hard ones, those that you miss frequently.

Do not permit any overweening desire to appear easy and graceful influence you, but shoot every shot with all your might. Put strength into the work first, and by and by grace will take care of itself. You are out to develop nerve force, and the only way to do that is to use what you have; rather than fire a shot indifferently, quit altogether. Nerve force can be developed by using it just the same as muscles are strengthened by being exercised.

CHAPTER V

SOME SHOOTING PSYCHOLOGY

PERHAPS the greatest weakness of the average field shot lies in his use of the second barrel. From my observations only the odd man can place his second charge with prompt accuracy, this being particularly true of the clay bird performers who from habit fire but one barrel. The observation applies with equal force to the ordinary sportsman, not one in ten of whom has a deadly second barrel. Having faithfully endeavored to ascertain the reasons for this, I will briefly set forth my conclusions.

The best second barrel shots that I have seen were men trained to live pigeon and wildfowl work, varieties of shooting more generally practiced twenty years ago than to-day. Live bird shooting at the traps is now generally forbidden by law, and the fowl are not distributed so widely as they once were. The pigeon shooter commonly fired both barrels at every bird, often for the sake of safety when the second charge was really not necessary to kill. The distance he was placed from the traps, from twenty-eight to thirty-three yards, made it imperative that he send in his loads with the utmost dispatch, a quick half-snap with the first and a rapid swing on with the second barrel. Then, too, under some rules the boundary was so short that the bird must be killed in the fraction of a second or it might fall out of bounds.

Trained to such conditions the pigeon shot cracked in his second barrel involuntarily, without a second thought or the least delay to verify the effect of the first charge. A hundred or even a thousand dollars might depend upon that second barrel driving in true and fast, the man who could not learn to place it in a quarter of a second soon dropping out of the game.

Though the shooting was from unknown ground traps, it was nothing unusual for a fast bird to be caught within twenty feet of where he sprang, and should the first charge fail the second would follow ere the pigeon had gone five yards farther.

Such rapid work as this is not absolutely essential on game, nevertheless it is the standard of excellence which the field sportsman should endeavor to attain. The gunner who cannot deliver his second charge in from a quarter to a half second after the first will not find that it avails him much, and as a rule he will fall into the common habit of letting the bird go after it has escaped the first pattern.

The wildfowl hunter is a good second barrel man also, and equally with the pigeon shooter from habit. These birds often fly in flocks which necessitates the use of both barrels; additionally many single ducks are struck without being killed outright which demands the use of the second barrel before the fowl can reach the water and dive.

While the wildfowler is not so sharp as the pigeon shot about pulling either his first or second load he is no less accurate and positive about it. Like the man of the traps, he knows before his piece comes to the shoulder that both barrels are to be fired, and hence there is never a delay in order to note what the first charge has accomplished.

The general run of upland shots go at the matter differently. Almost invariably they seem to believe that the first barrel will surely kill, the immediate brain impression when they see the bird still going on being one of surprise; recovering from this, they either fire the second barrel so quickly as to have practically no aim, or a slow, pottering second is sent in after the target is out of range. Either the unaimed or the pottering second charge is so generally ineffective that the gunner soon comes to depend entirely upon his first load.

Here is the trouble so far as I can analyze it. If the second barrel is to do perfect execution, the brain must complete its work *before the first shot is fired*. There is absolutely no time to think between the first and the second shots, the mind retaining barely sufficient control to prevent the shot going in when the bird is unquestionably a dead one. Indeed, in the case of pigeon shots, the barrel might be delivered involuntarily, whether the bird were dead or alive, this not altogether for safety as has been supposed, but rather because the finger was predirected to pull and there was no time to think or to stop it.

I have had the same thing happen to me in field shooting, when having made up my mind previous to delivering the first shot that the bird was a hard one and would probably escape, I could not avoid sending in the second barrel automatically after the bird was dead. This never happens except from brain orders that antedated the discharge of the first barrel. This is an extreme style of second barrel work, such promptness not being requisite in the field, but it is far more effective than the lame, halting method generally seen. So true is this that if I were coaching a novice in the use of his second charge

SOME SHOOTING PSYCHOLOGY 77

he would be required to pull it invariably alike when the bird was killed or untouched.

It follows from the foregoing that where the second barrel is to be made deadly there must be no pause in the aiming swing of the gun which should travel right along on the path of the bird's flight ready to be discharged the instant the gunner recovers from the recoil of the previous shot. The swing should be kept so true to the line of the bird's flight that in place of the arm hanging where first fired, it should be pointing within a foot or two of the target when the shooter has steadied himself sufficiently to aim again. On the other hand, having checked his piece, waiting to note the effect of the first load, the marksman will find his arm pointing so far from the bird that he either has to move the line of aim so rapidly that it becomes uncontrollable, or a slow swing will permit the game to get beyond range.

We will take the flight of a quail as an example. Should it break cover at twenty yards, it would on the average travel some forty feet before being fired upon, which would place Bob White distant thirty-three yards for the right barrel, delivered in less than a second. Now waiting to realize that the game has been missed would give the quarry another quarter of a second or fifteen feet; then, with a motionless gun, swinging on again from the previous point of aim will consume an additional half second, thirty feet, or a total of forty-five feet from where the first shot was fired, placing the quail forty-eight yards from the gun for the second barrel. On the contrary had the swing of the gun been maintained automatically the second shot should have been placed within twenty feet of the first, catching the bird when he was distant forty yards and still within reach of a good gun. None of the figures have been overdrawn and they can readily be verified by observing the efforts of sportsmen afield.

THE EFFECT OF RECOIL

It might be argued that it doesn't require the fourth of a second for the mind to realize a miss which the eye can see instantly. So it would not, except for the effect of shock upon the human brain, the shock of recoil. Furthermore, when the mind has just concluded a strenuous piece of work, like aiming and firing a gun, it pauses an instant before tackling a fresh problem. Combining this cessation of brain recording with the shock of recoil which causes the brain to cease acting entirely for a space of time, however small, and we have a loss of at least a quarter of a second—sometimes more. In fact so far has

SOME SHOOTING PSYCHOLOGY

the bird flown meantime that the gunner despairs of being able to reach it and so withholds his fire.

Recoil and its effects upon the shooter are worthy of careful study. It affects everyone, but in varying degrees. It has been observed that the most noted pigeon shots are men of strong physique, some of them seeming almost impervious to recoil, on the same principle that a pugilist might without blinking an eye take a blow on the jaw which would render an ordinary man unconscious. The jar of a shotgun's recoil and the blow of a fist differ only in the extent of shock and the time needed to recover. The shotgun may knock you out for perhaps not more than the tenth of a second, while the fist blow puts you away for ten minutes.

Nevertheless, no matter how hardy the constitution of the man, even a John L. Brewer, there is a shorter or longer space of time after a shot is fired when he can do nothing except he does it involuntarily, for the brain has been momentarily shocked into a state of coma. Notwithstanding this the nerves and muscles can be taught to accomplish orders given previous to this shock, maintaining certain actions automatically, or as we say from habit. The boxer does this when he starts a blow and sends it in after receiving such a jarring slap himself that he cannot remember when his own fist landed. If anyone doubts the effect of recoil shock upon the brain, let him try to recall the movements of his gun muzzle immediately subsequent to firing.

In the case of the writer his first distinct knowledge of where his gun is directed is when he finds it pointing below the target. Reasoning the matter out, he knows that the muzzle first flew up and then reacted downward, but from anything the brain has actually recorded it simply dropped below the point of aim. Accepting the foregoing as true we can see the need of acquiring a habit of maintaining the swing,—such an absolutely fixed habit as to require no direct brain control.

Flinching

However, the shock of recoil doesn't interfere with the work of a gunner so much as its anticipation, an anticipation that causes flinching and dodging before the shot is fired. Flinching after the recoil takes place would not merit much consideration, in fact would not be flinching. Flinching interferes so greatly with the delivery of both the first and second barrels, especially the latter, that we must analyze and give it full consideration.

The commonly accepted conclusion is that in

SOME SHOOTING PSYCHOLOGY 81

shooting flinching is due entirely to the fear of punishing recoil. It is supposed to consist of blinking, and dodging to such an extent as to deflect the muzzle, one man perhaps merely blinking while another dodges, or possibly blinks and dodges. My own conclusion is that flinching cannot in all cases be analyzed quite so simply as that.

Recoil undoubtedly is a prime factor in the trouble, but the sharp report of the gun has its influence also, for people with a tendency to flinch have noted an improvement in their work where a longer barrel was used, thus carrying the stunning noise farther away from the head. The loud report may cause more actual pain also than even the jolt of the butt stock. Mr. Roosevelt illustrates this in "African Game Trails" when telling how the heavy report of his elephant rifle caused bleeding of the nose and ears of a companion who stood beside him. It is claimed for the Maxim Silencer that it greatly lessens the inclination to flinch.

The above causes of flinching are obvious, but many flinch when shooting a 22 rifle which has neither recoil nor any undue noise. This might be ascribed to habit, but people dodge who are not in the habit of shooting at all.

Careful study of the matter has led me to believe that flinching is as much due to the strain of aiming and firing as any other cause. It requires a highly concentrated effort to hold either a shotgun or rifle perfectly steady and pull the trigger. The mind and nerves may not be able to sustain this strain for any great length of time, and certainly both are glad to be relieved of it as quickly as possible. Sometimes the brain gives up the task just an instant too soon, permitting the muscles to have their will of the piece, and of where it might afterward be pointed neither the eye nor the brain will take any cognizance.

Being overstrained, mind and nerves go on a strike, quit temporarily, making no further records until after the discharge takes place. Of whatever happens during this interim the shooter has no knowledge, though another man standing near can observe perfectly, and tell him, generally much to the gunner's surprise, and often little to his conviction. Whatever the eye might see, if the brain refrained from making any record, that particular thing never happened so far as the gunner's mind and memory are concerned. This is what renders it extremely difficult to cure flinching, the fact that so far as the marksman's own knowledge is concerned it never occurred. He did not know it and could not know it except

SOME SHOOTING PSYCHOLOGY 83

from the observation of others and a reasonable conviction based upon the effects of the shot.

Moreover the brain sometimes makes records with perfect clearness of things which never occurred. For instance, the shooter notes the speed of flight of the target, the velocity with which his line of sight is traveling to cover the mark, and calculates where he must hold in order to connect, but just at this instant the brain ceases to act, and the movements it has recorded as having taken place were never in fact accomplished. The result is a miss which to the marksman must always remain an absolute mystery.

The duration of time of which the marksman has no record, that is the space in which his brain is practically paralyzed, varies greatly with different individuals, though I am impressed with the belief that everyone is affected without exception. It might not last longer than the twentieth of a second, a time so short that it would have no practical influence upon the gunner's work, or it might have such duration as to make him very slow with the second barrel.

Moreover the mind may take cognizance of what is occurring without being able to take the initiative; it can note what is transpiring without having the power to give active commands. Afterwards the shooter can remember what took place and see where he missed an opportunity, but cannot tell why he failed to take advantage of it. We note examples of this kind in ordinary life; someone may neglect to act at a critical period and we say he lacked presence of mind—the shock caused a cessation of brain control. The brain may either not have been acting at all, or it may have been like the engine of an automobile that is pounding away with the clutch disengaged. In such an event, if muscles and nerves accomplish anything they must do it automatically; the machine could only go forward from previous momentum.

That is the point we are trying to drive home in shooting. For an infinitesimal or greater length of time when a shot is fired, the brain having lost control under shock, the muscles must be taught to carry on certain actions without conscious effort and yet with precision. There is no question but they can be trained to do this and it must be done if any great brilliance in marksmanship is ever to be attained. The greater the effect of recoil upon the gunner, the longer space of time in which the brain fails to function, the more thoroughly must nerves and muscles be taught to do things automatically, or instinctively, or unconsciously, call it what you will.

SOME SHOOTING PSYCHOLOGY

Could training of this nature be made perfect, the shooter might sight his target, throw up his gun to cover the bird, mentally calculate the point where it would be killed, that is where the line of aim and line of flight would connect, and then, all brain effort having ceased, the shot would be fired at the given point and the piece carried on to where the second charge was to be sent.

The writer has seen something similar to this accomplished numerous times in night shooting, the bird having shown only for an instant, giving its line and speed of flight, then disappeared utterly, but was killed with almost the same certainty as though it had been in plain sight. Naturally no second barrel could have been fired under such circumstances, because the result of the first barrel would not be seen, but had the gunner become aware in some way that he had missed, he might still have killed the bird with his remaining load, the whole mental effort being matured in the short space of time the bird was in sight.

The gist of this is that flinching, the cause of which is overstraining mind and nerves, can be cured by rigid training, but where the cause is an actual fear of punishment, either sound or jab, it is a different matter. The trite saying that prevention is better than cure applies with special force here. Had I the coaching of a lady or sensitive lad in shotgun shooting, no heavily charged twelve bore would ever be tolerated. I would choose a twenty gauge of more than normal weight, with barrels thirty or thirty-two inches long, and charge them lightly. Bad eggs are never so laid, but chemistry can do little for them after they have passed a certain stage; granting we have fair eyesight, nature has kindly endowed us with every power necessary to the making of a good shot, but very often indeed we foil her good intentions.

CONCENTRATION

Concentration is not a quality of an untrained mind. The expert shot may not know Latin, Greek, or mathematics, but his mind has been trained to concentrate more absolutely than would be needful in solving algebraic problems. Whatever his knowledge of gunnery, a man cannot be considered reliable with either rifle or smoothbore without the ability to fix his mind upon one thing to the utter exclusion of everything else in the world.

A rifleman who shoots upon the range with his fellows must so train himself that he will not hear the gun that is discharged within four feet of his head. The pigeon shot who could not prevent his mind from dwelling upon the previous misses would never excel in the sport. I have known two crack quail shots to cross their guns without knowing it when a bevy broke, and one of them shot off the muzzle of the other's gun. If, after selecting one bird of a bevy at which to fire, the marksman still sees other birds, the chances are that he misses them all. The shooter who can see trees that are liable to interfere with his aim would probably miss the target were the trees absent.

Some sportsmen cannot shoot well in company from inability to free their minds of some faint knowledge of what companions may be doing. When two men have both decided to fire at a bird, and the knowledge of what the other is to do is known to both, the bird will be more likely to escape them if but the one gun was fired—this because the minds of the gunners are divided between aiming and a consciousness of what the other gun is doing. One bird of a bevy is harder to kill than a bird rising singly for a similar reason. The match shooter who could feel an earthquake while aiming a shot would be the wrong man to place money upon.

A perfect control of the mind and nervous organization is essential to either field or trap-shooting, and the latter must hear what is being said about him without comprehending it. Making irritating remarks in connection with a competitor's shooting is an old trick of pigeon shots. The surest way to rattle a field shot is to induce him to discuss his misses while still shooting.

I remember one very clever quail shot that I took the job of rattling as a joke. His misses were usually shots that went low which caused him to fall into my scheme very innocently by agreeing that I should observe his work and call attention to every shot that went low. As soon as a bird arose I called, monotonously, " shoot high, shoot high." Very shortly he was missing nearly every bird fired upon and was a very thoroughly worried man. He afterwards told me that no sooner had the bird started than he could think of nothing but me and my infernal " shoot high."

Another individual was slow with his second barrel and I consented to coach him. He was a peppery chap, but usually pretty reliable with his first barrel. When the bird jumped, I said, sharply, " second barrel, second barrel," with the certain result of his rattling off both barrels without touching a feather. He flew into a rage finally.

A good shot with a trained mind, capable of

SOME SHOOTING PSYCHOLOGY 89

a high degree of concentration, would never have heard what I said. I have known men in brush shooting to strike their muzzles against a limb and push the branch along sufficiently to get an aim and kill the bird without knowing the limb was there until afterwards. With his mind divided a marksman can no more shoot straight than he could throw baseballs with both hands at the same time.

Here are a few axioms to be remembered: When aiming see nothing, feel nothing, hear nothing, think of nothing except the work in hand. While shooting solve the problem that is before you, and not the one that is past. Always kill the first bird shot at if you have enough loads in your gun, and never mind the others.

Self Confidence

In wing-shooting self confidence is a great asset. When a bird springs, if there is any doubt in your mind as to your ability to kill, the result will probably be a miss. A feeling must be ever present of absolute power to kill, a feeling born of previous success. Any feeling of confidence not born of past results is simply self deception. The vainglorious fellow who believes that he can do anything without trying has the sort of faith that wouldn't deceive anyone except himself.

If a novice could suddenly become miraculously possessed of the knowledge of exactly where to hold, with the mechanical ability to handle his gun, he yet could not shoot from lack of confidence in his newly acquired powers. The only self confidence built upon a solid foundation is that which comes from repeated, almost unvarying success. Confidence that comes from thoroughly tested ability is the stock in trade of the expert, and so long as he possesses it, he will shoot well.

Over confidence is a different matter—a miss usually resulting from the marksman's conscious or unconscious belief that it is not necessary for him to put forth his full powers. Shoot with all your might, at the easy birds and the hard ones alike, quitting when becoming tired rather than to shoot on carelessly.

CHAPTER VI

SPEED OF FLIGHT AND WHERE TO HOLD

NO amount of mechanical ability to handle a gun, such skill as might be acquired in trap shooting, will ever make a crack field shot out of the man who cannot estimate distances accurately, or who would not know where to hold if he did. In treating the subject of speed of mark, distance of target, and amount of lead, the writer feels constrained to admit that no theoretical knowledge can take the place of experience—a world of experience. The knowledge that comes only with long years of shooting is something that is never received on a platter of gold, but is bought and well paid for by the years that have gone by; it is power that was stored by the water that has gone past the wheel forever.

It is well that this is so, for if youth, with its irrepressible vitality, its muscles of iron and nerves of steel, might magically have the wisdom of age also, there would be no use for the veteran in this world—he would have to be Oslerized to make room. The best the author can do is to give such advice as may prevent the water from slipping by without turning the wheel.

Given the velocity of our projectile, the speed, distance, and angle on which our mark is traveling, and it is easy to work out the exact spot at which the aim must be taken in order to connect with the target. But, as has been shown in previous chapters, all our theories will be much modified and negatived by the different styles of shooting that men have acquired. Indeed so many factors have a bearing that it is rare for theory and practice to agree, and it is seldom that two skilled shots can be found who will not have divergent views about where to hold to get the bird.

Just how much the mathematical lead will have to be changed by the shooter's manner of swinging is something that everyone will have to decide for himself. The novice who manages by the rapidity of his swing to cut theoretical lead in half is on pretty safe ground. The scientific lead is given in these pages merely as a foundation for those who have not yet built a shooting structure of their own.

The following table gives either the estimated or timed speed of flight of some of our common game birds, taken when they are in full plumage and power, after having flown such a distance as to have acquired full momentum. It may be noted that birds of the order of quail and grouse are much more uniform in rate of progress than wildfowl. Nature did not give the grouse family such wing powers as the migratory birds, the one style of flying they have developed giving a very regular velocity. It might be taken as almost axiomatic that the greater the strength of wing possessed by any bird, the more will his speed vary with his humors and needs. Some hawks can stand still in the air, but they can also cut through it faster than anything that flies; the king bird ordinarily flies slowly, but he can do it like a flash of light when he wishes.

The variations in flight speed of quail and grouse can be ascribed to wind and atmosphere rather than to the will of the bird. One of them might fly past you, running a hazard of both barrels, without accelerating his wing strokes a particle, though doubtless he is as much frightened as any other bird. As much cannot be said of the duck tribe who sprint or loiter as the occasion demands, always appearing able to let out another link or two when danger is pressing.

The velocities here given are taken in feet per second rather than miles per hour, which is less readily comprehended or applied by the gunner.

TABLE OF FLIGHTS

BIRD	FEET PER SECOND	AVERAGE
Quail	65 to 85	75
Prairie Chicken	65 to 85	75
Ruffed Grouse	60 to 90	75
Dove	70 to 100	85
Jack Snipe	50 to 70	65
Curlew	45 to 65	55
Plovers	50 to 80	Accord. to variety
Crow	35 to 55	45
Mallard	55 to 90	75
Black Duck	55 to 90	75
Spoonbill	55 to 85	70
Pintail	60 to 100	80
Wood Duck	70 to 90	80
Widgeon	80 to 100	90
Gadwell	80 to 100	90
Red Head	110 to 130	120
Bluewing Teal	120 to 140	130
Greenwing Teal	100 to 130	115
Canvasback	130 to 160	145
Canada Geese	100 to 120	110

Brant, different varieties, average speed.....100

Some species of hawks have a speed of 200 feet a second.

There may be much greater variations in the flight of some of these birds than could be given in any table. An old mallard might plug lazily along, looking for a place to alight and not travel above thirty feet a second; on the other hand, he has a tremendous sprint when frightened. It might be said that given a good scare any of these ducks can reach maximum speed at will, and this sprinting flight is usually what the gunner has to make allowance for.

Give a bluewing teal a forty-mile breeze behind him, have the little rascal dropping down with it, and he comes on so fast as to be simply unhittable—some writers have claimed a speed for him of a hundred and fifty miles an hour or two hundred and twenty feet a second. The canvasback, redhead, and bluebill have a way of driving before a gale, too, that will be found fast enough in all conscience. Much of the fascination of wing-shooting comes from the fact that shots will always be afforded quite beyond the skill of mortal man.

On the contrary, many wildfowl are jumped, killed when hovering over decoys, or shot while unsuspicious of danger and moving slowly; enough of such shots are the rule to keep the tyro in good heart. Moreover, many birds like snipe, quail, chickens, and grouse are generally killed before they have attained full speed, perhaps ninety per cent. of such birds falling before they have reached normal flight velocity. Generally speaking, upland birds are not shot while passing the gun at right angles, but are going straight away, quartering, or twisting. It follows that in the fields our gravest shooting problems are other than reckoning speed or flight, but on the marshes our ability to calculate distances both horizontal and vertical has full play.

As a consequence wildfowl work may be said to be the most scientific wing-shooting in the world, while the expert of the uplands displays such uncanny quickness of perception that we can only explain it as instinct. Comparing the work of the men who follow either of these branches of sport, we might say that the sportsman of the fields has much to unlearn ere he can perform creditably upon the web-feet, and the man of the duck boat has only a foundation for partridge shooting skill. Having learned to kill quail, we can no more double up a whizzing canvasback than a man can play golf because he has learned croquet, or a ninety per cent. clay saucer breaker can hit a jack snipe.

Mathematical Lead

The figures given below are based upon a shot charge having a mean velocity over a fifty foot course of one thousand feet; over a one hundred

SPEED OF FLIGHT

foot range, of nine hundred feet; and for the distance of one hundred and fifty feet, eight hundred feet a second. Of course these calculations for shot velocity are only approximately correct, since they would alter with the size of the pellets, the larger shot maintaining a higher momentum at the longer ranges. Then, too, the initial velocity of the load might be greater or less than that given. Nevertheless, as it would be obviously impossible to work out the problems to fit every different charge, without taking up the space of a book, these will do as well as any.

No allowance has been made for the time required to pull trigger, the action of the lock, or the time necessary for the charge to pass from breech to muzzle, these being variable quantities that would only render the matter more complex. Mathematical lead, as here given, means simply the distance the bird would fly at its stated rate of speed while the shot were reaching it at the velocity mentioned.

A snipe, curlew, or plover, flying at the rate of sixty feet a second, would require a lead of two and a half feet at fifty feet; 5 5-9 feet at one hundred feet; and 9 3-8 feet at fifty yards.

A quail, prairie chicken, ruffed grouse, or mallard, covering space at a speed of seventy-five feet a second, would have to be led 3 3-4 feet at fifty feet; 8 1-3 feet at one hundred; and 14 feet at fifty yards.

A wood-duck, widgeon, or pintail flying ninety feet a second, would necessitate a lead of 4 1-2 feet at fifty feet; 10 feet at one hundred; and at fifty yards 16 7-8 feet.

A gadwell, greenwing, or wild goose traveling one hundred feet a second, would call for a lead of five feet at fifty feet; 11 1-9 feet at one hundred; and 18 3-4 feet at fifty yards.

A bluewing teal, canvasback, or redhead, passing at the rate of one hundred and twenty feet a second, would need a lead of 6 feet at a distance of fifty; 13 3-9 at one hundred; and at fifty yards 22 1-2 feet.

Should a canvasback or bluewing flash by at the rate of 150 feet a second, which they doubtless sometimes do in a wind, the lead for fifty feet would be 7 1-2 feet, that for one hundred, 16 2-3; for fifty yards 28 1-8 feet.

Granted that a hawk is able to fly two hundred feet a second, as stated, this means that over a fifty yard range the shot charge would travel but four times as fast as the bird, and the lead required to connect with him at the distance would be 37 1-2 feet. Even in the case of many of the ducks the shot have a velocity barely eight times as great as the target. Bearing this in mind, the need of correctly estimating distance and lead may strike the reader with new force.

It should be noted that these allowances for lead are all theoretical. The average experienced man, who fires with a rapidly swinging gun, would cut the given lead in half, and many expert wildfowlers would do better than that. It might be added here that any apparent lead greater than ten feet becomes pretty much guesswork. I have myself killed teal in a Minnesota gale by holding what I considered twenty feet ahead of them, but the feat was performed so seldom as to be readily recalled. It should be remembered that consciously giving a lead of twenty feet means really a much greater allowance if the gun is swinging true and fast. Naturally difficult shots like those are the "home runs" of wing-shooting.

It is hardly necessary to state that all the calculations here presented call for the bird's passing at right angles to the gun, any other angle of flight obviously changing the lead.

Judging Distances

Within shotgun range it is a comparatively easy matter to judge distances along the ground, especially stationary objects of recognized dimensions. Even birds a-wing that fly low nearly always pass a tree or something else that will afford us a basis for calculations. But with birds of unknown size, passing overhead, the matter assumes different proportions.

As previously stated, in upland shooting, where the birds generally rise near us, the matter of estimating distances need not concern us seriously. To be sure some shots will be missed through an incorrect lead due to badly judged flight, but such chances will not occur often enough to make a great difference in the size of the bag.

When wildfowl are in question, however, the subject is one that cannot be studied too closely. Ducks frequently maintain a line of flight so regular that striking them could present no great difficulty, if we knew how far they were away from the gun and exactly what lead to give them. Nine misses in ten upon the marsh are caused by faulty lead, which in turn must be attributed to poor judgment of distance or speed of flight.

Expert gunners estimate the distance of their mark, first, by knowing the kind of bird that is coming in and the size that it should appear at a given time. This makes it imperative that we should always be able to recognize the species of fowl that is approaching, be it teal, mallard, or pintail, for we cannot reckon nearness by size

SPEED OF FLIGHT

unless the size is well known. Secondly, the closeness of wildfowl can be approximately figured by keenly observing their markings. The shooter may say that he knew the bird was within range because he could see the white on its cheeks or the bars on its wings. The third method is to observe the apparent time required for the fowl to pass the gun. A bird that is well out will seemingly be much longer in passing than he would if he whistled by our heads.

One of the first things for a wildfowler to learn is to recognize the kind of duck which is approaching while it is yet at a distance. Until he can do this simply by the manner of the bird's flying he cannot hope to do a great deal of execution. This is true for more than one reason, but the particular one which concerns us now is the necessity for judging the bird's range by its size and appearance. The novice quickly comes to know that a mallard shows markings about as far as he can be killed, but if he is looking for trimmings of chestnut, white, and green, and a little black teal whizzes by at half gunshot he will never believe that it was within reach.

Nevertheless when experience has taught us to recognize at sight the different species of fowl there is no better key to the mysteries of unknown range than the markings of the birds. So many yards away we can distinguish the drakes from the ducks. A certain nearer approach and the chestnut and white of the mallard drake's breast no longer blend. Close up the very eyes of the bird may be seen, or the curl upon his tail, and then even the tyro knows that his mark is within easy reach.

Probably judging the distance of a wildfowl by his markings is the mode most commonly practiced. It is usually very reliable, though to be sure atmospheric conditions would have an influence. In rainy or foggy weather the colors might blend when the bird was nearly on top of you. And, by the way, estimating the distance or size of the flying game in a fog is almost impossible.

The apparent size of the mark also gives the gunner a very good line on its vicinity to the gun. When the bird looms up as big as a balloon you know that he ought to be within gunshot. It is here, however, that a man's eyes often deceive his reason. After killing a mallard at forty yards he permits a teal at thirty-five to escape because he fully believes it is out of range. In like manner, impressed with the appearance of the ducks, an old Canada honker will not seem to be half as far away as he really is, and a lot of forbearance is needed to keep from cutting loose while he is yet two gunshot lengths off. A safe plan with the big

SPEED OF FLIGHT

bird is to let him come just as close as he will, even if he drops into the pit. As a matter of fact that is a pretty good plan with any kind of a waterfowl, larger than a teal, for almost invariably they are not so close as they appear to be.

With very small birds the opposite might be true, as for example a quail at forty yards looks a long distance off, many would pronounce him from fifty to sixty yards away. This accounts for most of the sixty-yard shots on quail that we read about, the bird really being under forty oftener than not.

Judging the distance of the target by the rapidity with which it approached and passed the gun would be reliable if a man had his bump of mathematics highly developed and nothing else to do. The fowl being above our heads, with its markings showing clearly, should it seemingly require a long time to pass out of range, so that if need be a half dozen shots could be fired at it, we can safely assume that it was quite out of gunshot to begin with.

This reminds me of the efforts of a young friend of mine on his first duck shoot. He said that he had no trouble in getting an aim on some of the birds, but that others drummed by so fast that he couldn't shoot at them at all. I found that he was banging away at all the high flying flocks while the birds that whistled by his head escaped without drawing fire. In a modified way this happens to more than one novice.

Correctly estimating the distance of the mark will not avail us much unless we can at the same time closely calculate the speed of flight. The lead that would kill mallards right along will miss every teal that wings past us; or if by accident the beginner first learns to connect with the teal, he will be disgusted at missing the slow flying greenheads and pintail while apparently hanging right over his head. Indeed, the expert gunner is often dismayed to find that he cannot change his swing to adapt it to a slow moving mark after becoming accustomed to a speedy one. He perceives at once that he should do so, but shooting instinct and habit betray him. It is often laughable to see a crack shot lead a rabbit three feet too much when bunny hops up among the scattered quail. Knowing his bird, however, and its probable speed soon rights the matter, though undeniably a mixed bag calls for the highest degree of shooting skill.

The ordinary manner of estimating the lead for a bird is not in feet, as might be expected, but in lengths of the bird. For instance, at fifty yards ten feet appears a very short distance, but a bird that is known to be twelve inches long seems very small also; nevertheless by taking ten of his lengths we can safely assume that we are ten feet ahead of him. This rule of course pertains to any distance, while by attempting to work in feet

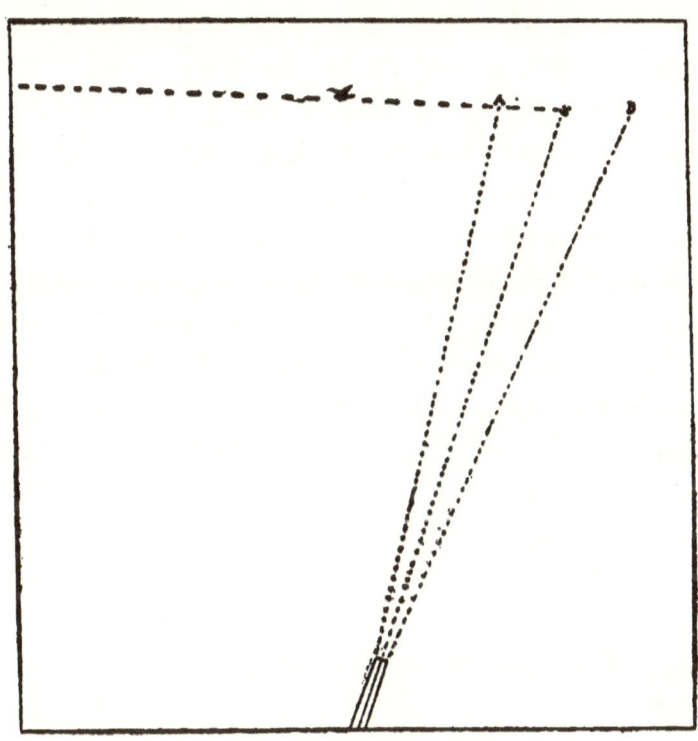

ESTIMATING DISTANCE TO HOLD AHEAD IN
LENGTHS OF THE BIRD

we will find that the eye will deceive us with every varying range. Not one inexperienced shot in a dozen can come closer than two feet to estimating the distance apart of two poles at fifty yards, not to mention measuring off ten feet in the air with nothing to serve as a guide or comparison. Despite this the novice may guess off ten lengths with sufficient accuracy to insure a kill.

After a time the final dependence of every veteran shot comes to be shooting habit. He glances at the flying quarry, swings upon it, and pulls when he feels he is right, with deadly results. The feeling of where to hold becomes so strong that no manner of reasoning or instruction would change his point of aim. This is not from any form of instinct, but simply because he swung so and killed many times before. He finally does it all without second thought, or first thought either, and should you ask him how much he led he wouldn't remember, either feet or lengths. Perhaps he might declare that he didn't lead at all, or barely shot in front; this because his mind was upon other things, as in swinging steadily and letting off at the exact time when he felt that was right.

Notwithstanding, this style of shooting can by no means be safely imitated by the novice. Humanity is so constituted that it must learn things slowly, through a process of reasoning, and reason only can lay a sure foundation for the so-called shooting instinct. If there is any royal road of success in wing-shooting the writer has never known anyone to strike it. Practice and study, practice and study; you will never become perfect, but you can become expert.

CHAPTER VII

HINTS ON SHOOTING DIFFERENT GAME BIRDS

THE limits of this book will not permit me to treat shooting the various game birds at length. Indeed, full instructions for handling the ordinary varieties of game which fall before the shotgun in this country would require a volume of itself. The best that I can do in this one chapter on the subject is to give a few hints which the beginner may find worth consulting.

THE BOB WHITE QUAIL

This little fellow is to head the list because he is the most widely distributed and best loved of all our game birds. In all the south, the west to the mountains, and throughout the Middle States, not a sportsman can be found who will not assert a fondness for quail shooting, the sport of many being limited to this one bird. The friendly brown chap ranges from Minnesota to the southern extremity of Florida, and in all this region the lad who has any shooting instinct born in him must have longed to follow the pointers and

HINTS ON SHOOTING GAME BIRDS 109

the quail, years ere he was able to bear the weight of a gun.

Little Bob affords shooting under many conditions, some of them so easy as to make him one of the least difficult of all our game birds to bag, and others quite hard enough to call forth the highest skill of the most expert gun. The tyro can kill some quail, and the practiced shot will fall far short of securing them all.

The marked characteristics of quail are that he lies best to the dog and rises nearer to the gun than any other game bird of the uplands; he is found both in the open and in heavy cover; he can be pursued on foot, on horseback, and sometimes in wagons; the bevies break away all in a bunch, with a tremendous rush and whir of wings, with a startling rapidity only rivaled by the ruffed grouse; and he is a winged athlete, capable of swerving and dodging when occasion demands in a manner to shame a jack snipe. Parenthetically permit me to venture here the opinion that quail do not dodge maliciously, their powers in this respect being merely called forth by circumstances.

In an open, level, ragweed field, where the vegetation is from knee to waist high, Bob sails away on an even keel, as straight as an arrow, whereupon a right and left should be within the powers of the average shot. However, let trees and brush intervene and the course of the little bird is beyond the foresight of man; then, too, he will swerve so quickly as to escape a charge of shot that has been sent direct for him.

One of the difficulties of quail shooting lies in the very fact that would apparently make his killing a simple matter, his rising near the gun. Let me illustrate: If a quail rose within ten feet of the gun and continued sailing around the shooter's head at a mile a minute gait, the chances are that he couldn't be killed in ten shots, both the bird and the gun changing angles with a rapidity beyond the ability of the mind to calculate. In the same way a close springing bird may change his angle with regard to the gun so rapidly as to entail a long and accurate swing before he can be covered.

He may rise within twenty feet of the gun, be killed within fifty feet, and yet meantime he has half boxed the compass. For such a shot as this the poise of the gunner's body must be maintained very nicely, if he is to turn half about without disturbing the balance, and at the same time cover a small, rapidly moving object with precision. This lengthy swing is a mechanically troublesome feat on the principle that anything at all hard to accomplish becomes more trying the longer continued. Making a long and accurate swing with

HINTS ON SHOOTING GAME BIRDS 111

a shotgun might aptly be compared with rifle shooting at a thousand yards. Any rifleman could hit the bullseye if you put him close enough, and the shotgun shooter could best place his charge upon the mark when he did not have to swing the arm at all.

The nature of the quail's flight frequently makes this long swing unavoidable. The bird may rise to the north, pass to the west, and be killed to the south. Had it been possible to foresee that the bird would swing about to the south before being killed, the gun might have been pointed there, rendering unnecessary a complex gun movement, but meantime the quarry would probably have gone in some other direction. The quail work that calls for care and skill is cover shooting, and the only safe rule there is to point your gun as near the bird as you can when he breaks and shoot as quickly as you can get on.

It is all well enough to give the trite advice not to shoot too quickly, give the bird time enough to straighten out, but half the time that this is done no shot will be fired at all. An old German hunting axiom covers this ground: "Any time you fail to shoot you have made a miss." We have all been out with the individual who withheld his fire because he "couldn't get on to that fellow," and he is a most exasperating companion where the other gun is waiting for him to shoot. The promptest possible work is requisite in quail shooting, the nerves of the gunner awaiting a rise being really keyed up as high as those of a sprinter on the mark listening for the pistol. A trained quail shot can be made to fairly jump into the air by roughly imitating the rush of the bird's wings.

This idea of waiting for a quail to fly a certain distance reminds me of the advice of dear old Frank Forester. His scheme was never to cock his piece until the bird was on the wing, then raise the left hammer, shift and pull up the right, by which time the shooter would have recovered his coolness, and the mark would be just the distance to be killed with ease and absolute certainty. I tried the plan when a boy, and can fully believe an old market gunner who said that Frank Forester never could shoot quail. The time to shoot a quail in the brush is when and where you can see him, the opportunity perhaps not lasting a quarter of a second.

The quail shot must possess mechanical steadiness, rapidity of action, nerve force, and nerve control. Mechanically there is no comparison between following, making a half turn, and cutting down a quail at fifty feet, and throwing up the gun with a five-inch swing to lead a mallard ten feet at fifty yards. Which of the shots will be the more difficult of accomplishment is a matter of training and experience. The quail shot must possess mechanics and nerve, the duck hunter, shooting knowledge. Personally I believe that quail work takes a great deal more out of a man, so that killing fifty quail will result in a nerve exhaustion that would not accompany bagging a hundred ducks.

Sporting writers are disposed to dwell upon the necessity for holding high in quail shooting, didactically stating that nearly all misses either go low or fall behind. Our literary gunners either get this idea from one another, accepting it without question as people do most of their wisdom, or their logic, so far as they have any, is that as the bird is rising from the ground, the charge must necessarily drop beneath unless care be taken to hold above. This theory really applies to pigeon shooting from the traps, originating from the demand of that sport.

The plain principle that should be remembered is that any bird flying away from the gun, beneath the line of aim, demands high holding whether or not the mark is rising; on the other hand, a target above the level of the eye may require low holding even when it is gradually rising. Let us make this plain. A bird rises near the gun and the weapon is pointed there, the muzzle being directed toward the ground. Now the mark may fly away nearly along the ground, as pigeons often do, and yet the line of aim must rise steadily until the gun is nearly in a horizontal position.

On the contrary, if the bird rises sharply at the first bound to a height some distance above the gun and then goes off level, or even rises somewhat, the gun will first be elevated to an angle of perhaps forty-five degrees and then with the receding target must drop until near the horizontal. Applying this principle, we find that shots must be directed high for all outgoing birds that are beneath the level of the eye and low for outgoing birds that are above the level of the eye unless they continue to rise at a very sharp angle.

I shall call attention briefly to the shots that are liable to go high; those in which the tendency is to fall under; the manner of flight when the charge often strikes behind; and where the error will be leading too much. To begin with permit me to repeat a statement previously made that in upland shooting only the occasional bird requires any great amount of lead. The obvious reason for this is that any target which rises close to the gun must in the nature of things go away from it and cannot maintain a right angled flight for any great distance.

HINTS ON SHOOTING GAME BIRDS

A bird may be readily overshot when he is flying straight away and perfectly level, in consequence of the line of aim being so very short. The gun comes to the shoulder pointing but a few inches beneath the target; then if it is brought up quickly the probability is that it travels above the mark while the trigger is being pressed. The problem of the shooter here is to start his line of aim sufficiently below the mark so that the finger can receive fair warning before the time comes to pull. Another shot often going high is when the bird rises to some little elevation and then drives away with a lowering flight before the aim is secured.

One of the most troublesome of open quail shots to gauge is when the little chap rises near the gun to a height of twenty or thirty feet and then goes off level. The natural inclination is to swing after him, unconscious that he is really going down toward the horizontal line and that the aim must in many instances be taken at least a foot low. Another quail shot in which few ever become proficient is the incomer. Flying low as this bird does, should he be allowed to approach within less than forty-five feet it is almost impossible to strike him owing to the rapidity with which the gun must be moved to keep pace with the flight. The nearer the bird comes to you the faster the muzzle swings, and at that the bird either outpaces you or you jerk ahead blindly without any aim and kill only by accident. The incomer should be fired upon when fifty feet or more away should he be seen in time, or failing to get in the shot there, turn on the bird and take him after he passes by. When attempting this last feat always hold under such a distance as would appear a sure miss, usually a foot and a half unless the bird is rising.

Naturally the shape of a man's gunstock will modify his holding for any of the shots that should go high or low. This particular flight, the bird passing overhead and going away, was the most successfully accomplished with the use of one peculiar weapon which the author owned fifteen or twenty years ago. It was a straight stocked gun to begin with, made emphatically so by the addition of a Monte Carlo comb which caused it to shoot high and to the left. With this piece there was never any of the trouble with the incomers that I have experienced with other arms. The incomer was allowed to pass and then the aim taken about two feet low and four inches to the right, and down he came stone dead, seemingly the most certain shot that could possibly be taken.

Shot charges should be delivered high when the

game rises so wild as to require snapping before reaching the end of its climbing bound, the snap shot being demanded to prevent the quarry getting beyond range. Under such circumstances the line of aim would not follow the line of flight, but would pass straight up in front of the mark to the connecting point. Such shots as this more often occur in prairie chicken shooting than with quail.

Another problem that necessitates quick perception is when the bird meets some obstruction to his flight. The inclination of a quail is always to jump over rather than dodge under anything that comes in his way, the rise beginning some distance before he reaches the obstruction. Hence watch your mark closely should he be winging toward a low tree or brush for he is nearly certain to rise, and it is then a safe rule to hold over anyway.

It should be known that the majority of under shots are due, not so much to the flight of the bird, as to the nerves of the gunner. When there is need of quick action, in a semi-snap or rapid swing, with the sportsman's nerves tensely strung, there is more than a possibility of the finger betraying the judgment by letting off before the piece has quite traveled up to cover the mark. In every instance of this kind the charge must either go low or behind, and usually both.

Take it for granted that in upland shooting two-thirds of the misses that fall beneath and back are the result of rebellious nerves. Nerves are especially hard to manage where the swing is a long one, as we have shown it must often be with quail; hence the pigeon shooter's axiom of "shoot high and in front" might apply to Bob White, only it should read "don't pull until you are on." If you cannot avoid doing this, harden the trigger of your gun.

Individuals differ, and the personality of the gunner must always govern largely, but the writer has always had his best success in quail shooting by firing a semi-snap shot with the first barrel and swinging after with the second. With practice too it will be found that the gun can be swung with greater ease and certainty, and a better view maintained of the mark when the head is held upright, free of the gunstock.

Prairie Chicken

Chicken shooting was once such a simple business as scarcely to deserve the name of sport, for the half-grown chicks were killed in August while still under charge of the old hen. At present the hunting of these grouse begins with October, and the work upon the mature and powerful fowl is not only elegant sport, but of a nature to test the skill of any man. The bevies now become broken up, scattering about singly, in pairs, and small bunches, and then with the approach of winter packing into coveys of several hundred. The larger the packs or the colder the weather, the wilder chickens become and the more difficult the work of the gunner.

The very finest of prairie grouse shooting is to be had on the occasional warm, sunny days that come in November and December. Then while the big fellows are not tame, and certainly not tame shooting, they will frequently permit the gunner to approach within half gunshot, and a half dozen of the powerful birds in the strength of their lusty growth and the beauty of their winter plumage will afford intense satisfaction to any sportsman who prefers quality to quantity. We will treat of bagging these strong, brown fellows rather than the September fledglings that even the tyro would require no special instruction to kill.

The full grown pinnated grouse is rather more powerful of wing than a quail, though from his size he seems to move slower. He is, however, not so sharp in getting away from the mark as his little cousin, and hence if he lay to a point like the latter would be easier shooting. But the late fall chicken doesn't lie as close as a quail, the rise being anywhere from twenty yards to a long gunshot. It follows that straightaway chances are the exception rather than the rule, and the distance of the spring makes it needful that nearly every shot be well judged and given its proper allowance ahead. Almost invariably daylight should be seen between the point of aim and the bird, the lead being anywhere from a foot to eight feet where an old cock is crossing at forty-five yards.

In the course of a day upon the prairies nearly every description of shot known in wing-shooting may be afforded. Occasionally a bird will rise under your feet and drive away low over the short coated prairie, but the majority will be quartering shots at every conceivable angle from a straight-away to a direct incomer. Frequently the cackling chaps will spring to a height of thirty or forty feet, and then drop away with whip and twist and flash of wings toward the distant horizon—the most careful gunner finding plenty of empty space along these curves of flight. Numbers will cross at right angles, demanding as much lead as a mallard duck, and sometimes a pack will come stringing along like English driven

HINTS ON SHOOTING GAME BIRDS 121

game, yielding the sportsman as hot a thirty seconds as he ever experienced.

The chicken, being a heavy bird, cannot reach top speed so promptly as a quail, and they have a way of climbing for the first few yards that keeps them within gunshot when a quail or ruffed grouse would be putting such space between himself and the gun that shooting at him would be useless.

I should estimate that a quail would fly forty-five feet the first second after his jump, a ruffed grouse from forty-five to fifty-five feet, a chicken perhaps not above thirty, though in doing this he might rise to a height of twenty feet. As a consequence pinnated grouse can sometimes be bagged that take wing forty yards from the gun, but it calls for a high degree of shooting skill to gauge both his speed away from the gun and his angle of elevation. With these long range shots the gun should always come up to the point of discharge with the least possible lost motion, something of accuracy being sacrificed to prompt delivery of the charge, care being taken to shoot plenty high —sometimes as much as two feet above the climbing fowl. This work has more resemblance to jumping ducks than anything quail shooting develops.

The mature chicken is suspicious, preferring

rather to trust to the strength of strong wings than to any ability to hide. With the wild fellows it is better to chance a miss with a rough snap that has power to drive the pellets home in place of a precise aim that could only rattle the shot upon his stiff wing feathers. Nevertheless, I have found the quick half snap to be the most killing style, care being taken to steady the gun before lifting it to the mark.

The second barrel will naturally follow the first in a quick swing and should snap in after the first with the same celerity as in pigeon shooting from the traps. The best policy in all wing-shooting is to consider any bird near enough for the second barrel that was within reach of the first. Otherwise an indecisive second barrel will grow upon you to the great detriment of all your shooting.

Where the utmost rapidity is requisite the obvious thing to do is to get your weapon to shoulder with the flash of the springing bird; then in the slight interim needed to steady the piece the calculation for lead can be made and the charge sent there instantly, care being taken not to jerk the weapon with uncontrollable roughness. With the shooter walking up his bird, without having gun, legs, or body in shooting position, a grouse can be stopped by a fast man within five yards of

HINTS ON SHOOTING GAME BIRDS

where it breaks cover, the time taken to accomplish all the separate, complex movements not being over half a second.

Only the wisest old chicken dog will be found serviceable on November grouse, an animal which can scent his game at from fifty to two hundred yards, one that will not attempt to approach it except in close company with the gun. On birds that have packed and become excessively wild, two men may often work together to advantage, the one hiding in the grass while the other drives the game over him.

There are times when not a single chicken will permit an unconcealed gunner to approach a foot within one hundred yards. Under the circumstances the only recourse is either to drive the birds or to endeavor to shoot them from horseback or wagon. A horse can sometimes be galloped right among the fowl, especially in a country where they have become accustomed to the unmolesting cowpuncher. A driven wagon sometimes proves equally serviceable, but the second time you endeavor to drive up to a flushed pack you will learn that the wise birds have sized up the situation perfectly, and chickens can fly about over the rough prairie faster than horses can trot.

The Ruffed Grouse

The ruffed grouse is the wisest of all his tribe, of which all have brains, and as a winged sprinter is the quickest away from scratch of anything that flies. The quail dodges with phenomenal suddenness when anything obstructs his path, the wind sometimes unbalances a jack snipe, giving his flight the acme of eccentricity, but the partridge does it all deliberately and maliciously. With gunner and ruffed grouse, as with pitcher and batter, it is a guessing game and whichever outguesses comes off victor.

Flush a quail in the thick woods and should there be an opening he may fly straight down it; a partridge might, too, but be sure he will not. I have seen one of the birds sitting before a dog's point in a perfectly open spot, but there was a tree within twenty feet. I planned to get a shot at him before he could reach that tree, and ordered the dog to draw in while I stood with gun ready. The wise old scoundrel got up with provoking deliberation, spread his tail, legged it around behind the tree, and then took wing with a tremendous hurrah.

In partridge shooting, knowledge of the bird's habits will avail more than shooting skill. The hunter should have that rare sort of partridge wisdom that few are born with and fewer ever acquire. One can always luckily select the spot where the fish will bite if there are any, and the old partridge crank can forever place himself in just the spot to get his opportunity while all the other fellows have to take what happens to come.

The thing for the ruffed grouse hunter to do is to shoot and never count shells. Should the bird fly behind a tree and not reappear shoot the tree in two if you can. When he simply roars in beyond the limbs, make no hesitation for that is the very place to kill him. Swing along on the line of flight, so much of it as you have seen, take it for granted that he is still going the same course at the same rate of speed, and when you know you are right pull with as much confidence as though the bird were yet in plain sight. Then listen for the bird to fall—and sometimes he will. If he doesn't, simply blame the limbs; they have no shooting conceit to be aggrieved. Seeing sparkles and flashes of light, glinting through the woods, left there by the partridge's wings, shoot as far ahead as your conscience will let you, and more than likely another bird will be added to the bag.

In the rare times when you catch a ruffed grouse in the open, as in little isolated clumps from which he must fly, or along old, overgrown fencerows, he is no more difficult target than a quail or chicken. He is quicker away from the gun in heavy cover, but in full flight has no greater speed than either of the others. Generally no great amount of lead need be taken, but the shots he affords are of such diversified character that there can be no such thing as systematic partridge shooting. The marksman must simply suit his style to the nature of the shot as it comes. At the odd times when an easy shot appears, make sure of that bird, with all the precision and steadiness possessed, for he is the bird that should add weight to the back coat pocket.

When there is but a ten foot opening in the trees snap the bird there, no matter what the odds against a kill; that is where the fun comes in and the rare pleasure of a kill that happens seldom. The ruffed grouse, by the way, is the only bird upon which the ethics of sportsmanship should tolerate the use of a cylinder bored gun. When this bird is killed fairly upon the wing I should not feel disposed to lecture the man who used a bell muzzled piece.

Like the grouse hunter, the partridge dog just happens to be one. If nature hasn't done a great deal for him, man can do little. Training can teach the dog to hunt close to the gun, to flush to order, and to be stanch, and then he may or may not be a partridge dog.

It is well to hunt ruffed grouse with a reliable companion, one that can be depended upon not to shoot you first and feel sorry afterwards. The right kind of a hunting partner will enable both guns to secure better results, since the second gun will often get its chance while the wily bird is outmaneuvering the other. Further advantages, such as marking the birds, will be obvious without dwelling upon them.

Next to purely open shots the easiest partridge problem is when the bird is climbing through the thin limbs or just as he tops the undergrowth; the hardest is where he drops, like a bullet, out of a tree and skims the ground. One partridge killed in three shots is good shooting; fifty per cent. on quail is of about the same order, and three out of four chickens.

Snipe Shooting

The writer once hung a jury because he knew the other eleven fellows were wrong. They wished to clear a man of the charge of murder who had shot another in the back, the plea being self defense. Utterly regardless of the risk of being in a minority of one, I propose to maintain now that snipe are the easiest to kill of all our common game birds with the exception of the rail which at best doesn't deserve to be listed as game. That the snipe is a difficult shooting proposition seems to be one of the popular sporting errors that appear to have been accepted as an inheritance. Naturally the fiction writer and the book learned gunner perpetuate the error, considering themselves on safe ground when dwelling upon the difficulties of snipe shooting.

It is true that jack sometimes flies very erratically on windy days when he finds trouble in balancing himself while gaining sufficient momentum to progress steadily. Like other birds, too, his temper is affected by cold, raw weather, or when he is hungry and food scarce; at such times he has little hesitation about getting up well out of range and leaving promptly for some more genial snipe world. When flushing wild it is quite a literal statement of fact that snipe are hard to hit, for if tied to a post out of gun range not many would be hurt. It appears, too, that a snipe really requires some ballast of fat if he is to sail upon an even keel, the thin little chaps surprising themselves with aerial gymnastics in the wind.

But in actual snipe weather, warm sunny days, with cover good and food plentiful, jack snipe

HINTS ON SHOOTING GAME BIRDS

shooting is little more of a feat than smashing clay birds, than which there is no simpler shotgun work with which to compare.

The statement often made that the shooter should always withhold his fire until the bird is from twenty-five to thirty yards distant is the height of absurdity. The same shooting principle applies to snipe that holds with any other game bird, catch him before he becomes hard. When these birds are lying well to the dog and gun they get up lazily and float away with long, easy bounds. The first jump may carry his snipeship twenty feet, and then with a twist of his body he covers half a dozen yards at a more or less acute angle, but at the end of one of these aerial leaps the bird hangs for the fraction of a second and there you can almost catch him with a rifle bullet.

The preliminary spring with accompanying saucy " scaipe " should warn the gunner and the end of the next leg of the zigzag ought to find poor jack ready to be smoothed down and placed in the bag, the man of ordinary quickness striking his mark inside of sixty feet or not over forty-five from where it broke cover. The motion of a snipe is really something like that of a skater who shoves out first upon one foot and then the other, the bird, however, making longer and quicker strokes, which become very choppy when he is sprinting.

There is a bit of up and down movement to the flight of a snipe under some conditions, but not a great deal, and when he is passing or circling the gun, the in and out motion is little in evidence and he flies practically as level as other birds. When going straight away his criss-cross style is most apparent, and such shots are the hardest in consequence. It is this feature of his flight that makes hunting down wind the most effective, since the bird has a preference for rising against the wind, and will then beat back, affording a crossing shot, while should the shooter walk up wind his target would likely be a straightaway. Nevertheless up wind or down wind, should the quarry rise within twenty yards he cannot escape without hazarding both barrels, one of which will generally suffice.

The movements of a snipe should never be followed by the line of aim. To do so would render his flight as hard to solve as sporting literature has pronounced. Get the gun up pointed under him and then snap ahead on one of his long bounds before he can tack. The thing is so easily done that I will leave it to any experienced snipe shot if there is any great feat about cutting down twenty of the little beauties straight.

HINTS ON SHOOTING GAME BIRDS

Indeed this bird is one that calls for a hunter's forbearance in the matter of bag. Some years ago immense bags of snipe were common. The record so far as I know was something over six hundred birds killed by a Louisiana planter in one day. In the vicinity of St. Louis two hundred snipe a day were not considered shooting worthy of special note, and no snipe were in unless fifty could be killed. To-day twenty-five longbills should be considered the limit per gun, though the number may be secured in a few hours' shooting over favorable ground.

Jack is the gentlest and most unsuspicious little vagabond in the world. Should you miss him he will pitch about for a few minutes, perhaps to settle down again within fifty yards of the gun for another hazard with the death whistling lead.

A clever shot on snipe should account for eighty per cent. of the birds shot at, a performance not to be expected with any other upland game bird. They are not only a simple proposition to hit but are easily killed which permits the use of lightly charged and small gauge weapons.

WILDFOWL SHOOTING

Duck shooting is the billiards of work with a

scatter gun. The uniform flight of the fowl, the absence of any interference with the aim, preparedness of the shooter from having been given due warning of the approaching bird, tend to place every factor of the shooting problem at the gunner's command. Always, however, the hunter's skill and experience must equal the demand, the whole situation resolving itself finally into a knowledge of where to hold. In quail shooting a man's difficulty lies in being unable to place his charge to the spot which he knows is right; in duck shooting the main question is where to point the gun, the pattern being readily sent to the estimated lead. It is nearly as easy to direct the aim ten feet in front of the mark as two feet, always provided you know it should lead ten feet and not two or six. Therefore conclude that every successful shot must be made with an absolutely correct estimate of speed of flight and distance of mark. When this can be done with regularity the pleasure of verifying the judgment with a long, clean kill is superior to that connected with any other style of shooting.

The most that I can do here is to call attention to some of the various shots which the wildfowler will be called upon to solve as primary lessons in the duck shooting game.

The overhead, incoming shot is made by throwing the gun beneath the target and pitching it rapidly upward until it passes the bird, firing the instant the mark is quite hidden by the barrels. Little conscious allowance ahead will be found necessary in making this shot, but the speedier the mark the more rapidly the gun should be swung. It can be readily understood that with a rapidly moving muzzle a greater lead will be taken automatically at a long distance than a short. In any event it has been found in practice that swinging the gun from beneath to cover and hide the mark will usually result in a kill. This is probably the easiest shot made in duck shooting for the first barrel.

No sooner, though, has this first load been fired than the second charge has its work cut out for it. Many species of ducks will tower with the bang of the gun, maybe rising straight into the air or even beating back upon the course they came. In consequence the left barrel, if not sent in promptly, will have to be fired well above and possibly, paradoxical as it may seem, behind the duck, considering the route it was traveling when the right was pulled. Most likely the scared flock will merely sheer off, mounting at the same time, and the new angle of flight must be instantly reckoned with if the shot is to go home.

A duck that is coming at a high clip which he deflects into a sheering, curving tower is about as hard a nut to crack as comes under the wing-shooter's mallet. One half second may take the mark out of range, and a man's thinking apparatus must work fast. Certain other varieties of duck, like the bluewing teal and the canvasback, will not flinch or tower, but continue directly on with redoubled speed. Now the bird will pass the gun which must turn on him, affording quite a different shot from the other. Then in order to lead the hold must be low—well under—sometimes as much as three feet, but the farther the mark is allowed to go the closer it is covered, since with distance it comes more directly into the line of fire and the charge is sent more closely in the line of flight.

Many birds passing well out will also swerve and rise with the report, which necessitates a lessening of the front lead to direct the second charge higher. A certain duck might be killed by shooting eight feet ahead of him, but to kill his mate with the second barrel it should go only two feet in front and two feet high. On firing the right barrel an experienced shot ought to be able to foretell pretty well what the remainder of the flock would do by knowing the species of fowl. The acme of duck shooting is to make

HINTS ON SHOOTING GAME BIRDS

both shots tell, the indifferent performer frequently being effective with the first.

It will usually be discovered that birds which pass to the right call for a greater lead than those flying to the left, because a right hand gunner swings less freely and rapidly in that direction. In the case of the writer, a third more lead must be given when swinging to the right. Of course the opposite would be true were the shooter left handed.

The surest double is to be made while the birds are approaching the gun, never permitting them to pass by. Turning to shoot in a restricted blind is trying, and more so from a duck boat. If the ducks are close up take the leader first, but if farther out select the rear fowl and those closer up can hardly escape being shot at. There is room for coolness and good judgment in this. Should you choose the leading bird and fire too quickly, those behind him may climb out of reach, while trying for a rear fowl after they are well in may force a difficult turn on the others.

A descending bird is a hard shot, both by reason of his increased speed and because a gun cannot well be swung down, and the descending line of flight must be met by a still gun, as in snap shooting, causing a loss of all the advantage of swinging with the target. A rising bird is far easier, and hence it is well in decoy shooting to pull just as the fowl is hovering to alight, or take him in his upward climb away from danger.

In jumping ducks close study should be given as to the variety of fowl we are starting. A mallard usually climbs nearly straight upward, a shot just in front of the bill should get him. On the contrary a teal scurries off low along the marsh, and the holding must be well ahead and only a trifle high. A widgeon makes one great bound upward and then goes off at a sharp angle. If quick enough the hunter's surest shot on the widgeon is at the end of this leap when the duck will be about ten feet high. Any dwelling upon the aim here is fatal, since the bird will change his line of flight acutely, and a long swing will have to be made after the speeding mark.

A pintail climbs and gradually bears off, at the same time circling the gun. When jumped he is one of the easiest birds to kill, because of this circling habit which keeps him within range of the gun for such a length of time. A greenwing teal behaves very like a mallard but is quicker in action. It is seldom that any except fresh water ducks are killed by jumping them from the edge of a marsh.

CHAPTER VIII

Clay Bird Shooting

IN this chapter on clay bird shooting no pretense of giving expert instruction will be made. The man who is desirous of going up against our skilled professionals at tournaments must receive his teaching where alone it can be given in a practical form, at the open meets where none are barred.

The average, ambitious young marksman can become a winning trap shot if his ambition, staying qualities, opportunities, and finances will stand the strain. However, the man who would attain winning tournament form has set for himself a herculean task these days. At a rough guess I should estimate that there are a hundred thousand men in America who do more or less trap shooting, and of these there may be twenty real cracks among the amateurs and as many top-notch professionals. In professional trap shooting there isn't much room, even at the top, with a deuce of a strenuous road getting there.

The usual process of schooling and graduating

is something like this: The youngster with the good eye, steady nerve, and strong physique must practice with his home club until he can lick all his mates to a frazzle. His preliminary work should be under the most trying conditions possible, throwing his birds as far as the traps will send them, granting his companions handicaps of from two to four yards, and shooting generally at unknown angles. When he can smother just about everything he shoots at, has found a gun and load exactly adapted to himself and the work, and has reached a form which he considers unbeatable, then he is in shape to attend a big shoot.

When he does that he should make up his mind to begin with that he is not going to win, not going to come anywhere near winning. In fact, the great lesson before him now is to learn to lose with equanimity, without becoming rattled or discouraged. It is proverbially easy to run a winning race, the only kind he has been accustomed to heretofore, but now he must learn to keep a stout heart when back in the ruck, when he is not only being beaten but distanced. The novice may have skill, but he will run up against equal skill, combined with experience, trained nerves, and a phlegmatic philosophy that accepts things as they come. There never was a man so good that he couldn't be beaten, and if he allows that to worry him defeats will become the rule. However, the beginner can console himself with the knowledge that the hardened old sinners who are now licking him to a standstill have been through the very course of sprouts they are treating him to; they survived it and so can he—if he is exactly built for the game.

I make no doubt but our great clay bird shots are the most skillful gun-pointers that the world has ever known. I am saying this advisedly, remembering the scientific work of military marksmen, the hairsplitting accuracy of scheutzen riflemen, the deadliness of the modern big game hunter, the skill of the pigeon shot, or the instinctive, inexplicable performances of the snap shot afield. No other class of marksmen has ever made the same determined effort to acquire gun skill—it is no uncommon thing for the artificial target shot to fire two hundred cartridges, day after day, and sometimes a thousand rounds in a single day. Such an effort, intelligently applied, is bound to result in extraordinary proficiency, and it does. At the present time a score of a hundred straight fails to attract a passing glance, and ninety-five per cent. for an entire shooting season wouldn't set the shooting world afire.

Nowadays there is a craze for high scores and wonderful averages. The most unfortunate thing about this is that the ordinary shot becomes discouraged if he shoots below ninety, and as a consequence the management of shooting tournaments have been forced to make the shooting conditions too mechanical and too easy. Birds are thrown with but moderate force, and with the greatest uniformity. The angles of flight are never very sharp, never varying from the straightaway enough to require or develop good judgment in leading. Moreover, the butt of the gun is held to the shoulder before calling "pull," and the gunner knows exactly when and where his bird is to be sprung—all of which tends to high percentages without being especially good practice for field work.

However, trap shooting is an excellent sport, entirely aside from any desire to shine as a fixed star. Congenial company, the merry crack of nitro powder, the elation that comes from problems attacked and mastered, the competition that is sharp without bitterness, are equally possible for us all, the good, the moderate, and the indifferent.

Individuals and small clubs that shoot for sport, or as a means of increasing skill which will be useful in field work, need not confine themselves to hard and fast rules, especially as regards manner of throwing the targets and handling the gun. The man who desires to acquire facility and deftness in the use of his weapon had better not place it to his shoulder before calling pull, as is now the universal custom among trap shooters. It is much better to hold his gun as he would when expecting the rise of wild game, taking his chances of missing through not bringing the arm to his shoulder properly just as he would be obliged to do in any other description of wing-shooting.

Nothing calls forth so much criticism from the field shot as to see a man standing before the traps stiffly, his gun glued to his face. Such a style is utterly inimical to all grace of action, and moreover it is a manner of handling the gun that proves useless in any description of wing-shooting barring clay birds. Standing up all fixed, cocked, and primed, with the gun muzzle pointing very nearly to the spot where the piece is to be discharged is something that surely has to be unlearned when the gunner attempts legitimate wing-shooting.

I have seen a trap shot trying to walk up quail with the butt of his gun to his shoulder in its customary trap shooting position, and, to put it in a feminine way, he looked a sight—neither could he shoot. The old rule of gun beneath the elbow until the marksman called pull is much better, always provided the gunner is trying to learn wing-shooting and not clay bird smashing for a record.

It occurs to me that the clay bird and trap can be much better used in teaching shooting on the wing than it ever has been. The man who is desirous of learning to swing and to lead his mark such a distance as is often needful in wildfowl work, cannot expect to be taught this by practicing exclusively at straightaway and easy quartering birds. Neither is there any reason why he should not have his birds thrown at any desired angle to the gun, as will be noted in the chapter on Primary Lessons. Even clubs which ordinarily are obliged to shoot under the rules of the Interstate will find it an attractive change to try the game occasionally; one man up and birds thrown at widely varying angles.

The ingenuity of the marksman will readily suggest shots that approach field conditions. Beware of high flung birds which rise and hang in the air; they are no better practice than old tin cans tossed up.

Of course all this sort of thing implies that there shall not be too many guns at work and is especially adapted to country clubs and small shooting parties. Where clubs embrace a number of gunners, as they usually do in the city, or when time is a factor, it will be necessary to follow trap shooting rules pretty closely in order that everyone shall have a fair amount of practice and a like opportunity.

The man who desires to compete at tournaments or club shoots should be conversant with the trap shooting rules of the Interstate Association. Space in this chapter will not permit me to give these further than instructions for placing the traps and throwing the targets. However, the rules will be sent to anyone who applies to the secretary.

Formerly trap shooting was from either three or five traps, set three to five yards apart, sometimes in the segment of a circle, at others in a straight line. The traps were screened of course and the birds might be thrown from unknown traps and unknown angles, known traps and unknown angles, or known traps and known angles.

However, the rules of the Interstate Association call for either a single automatic trap, or three traps, set four feet apart (which amounts to practically the same thing as one, since the shooter knows where his bird is to rise). For manner of throwing the birds, I cannot do better than quote from the booklet of the Interstate Trap Shooter's Association.

FLIGHTS AND ANGLES

"Targets, whether singles or doubles, shall be thrown not less than forty-five yards nor more than fifty-five yards, with a flight between six and twelve feet high at a point ten yards from the trap. Except in double target shooting, the flight of targets shall be at unknown angles, thrown within an area of forty-five degrees right and left of an imaginary straight line drawn through the center of number three firing point, and prolonged through the center of the central trap or through the center of the single trap where one is used. In single target shooting, to aid in distinguishing targets within and without bounds, four stakes, not less than three feet in height, shall be placed in the arc of a circle whose radii are fifty yards and whose center is the center of the central trap or the center of the single trap where one is used. Respectively right and left of the aforementioned straight line, two of the stakes shall be placed upright, one at forty-five degrees and one at sixty-five degrees in said arc."

DOUBLES

"Each double shall be thrown as a right and

left quarterer, whose flight shall be limited to the two areas between twenty and sixty-five degrees right and left of an imaginary straight line drawn through the center of number three firing point and prolonged through the center of the central trap or through the center of the single

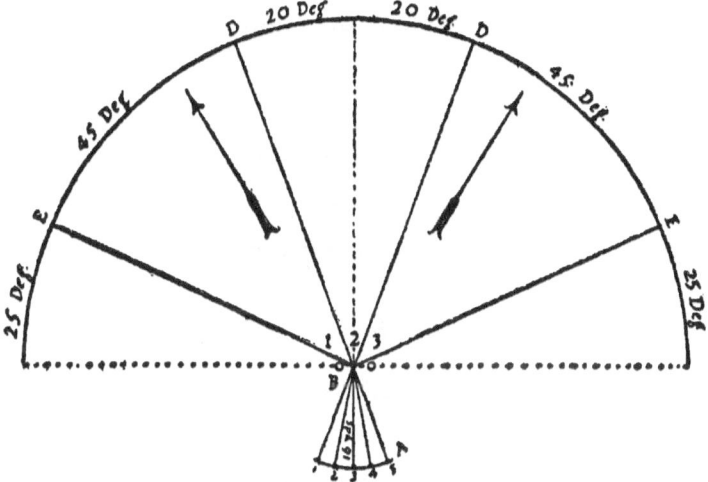

ARRANGEMENT OF FIRING POINTS IN REFERENCE TO TRAPS

trap, where one is used. To aid in distinguishing between the targets within and without the bounds, four stakes, not less than three feet in height, shall be placed in the arc of a circle whose radii are fifty yards, and whose center is the center of the central trap or the center of the single trap where one is used. Respectively right and left of the aforementioned straight line

146 WING AND TRAP-SHOOTING

two of the stakes shall be placed upright, one at twenty degrees and one at sixty-five degrees."

PITS AND SCREENS

"Pits and screens shall be used to protect the trappers. The screens shall not be higher than is necessary for such protection.

FIRING POINTS

"The firing points shall be three to five yards apart in the circumference of a circle whose radii are sixteen yards (see diagram).

DISTANCE HANDICAPS

"The distance handicaps when used shall be on the prolongation of lines given in diagram one, commonly known as 'fanshaped.' The distance between the firing points at sixteen yards shall then be nine feet." (See diagram.)

I cannot quote further from the rules of the Interstate, but provision is made for squads of five guns which are to face the trap from positions marked 1, 2, 3, 4, and 5, all the firing points being equally distant from the central trap and consequently in the segment of a circle whose diameter is thirty-two yards.

Under old trap shooting rules a 12 gauge gun

was placed at sixteen yards, a 10 gauge at eighteen, 16 gauge, fourteen, and 20 gauge, thirteen, but the Interstate makes no provision for any gun other than a 12. A shooter may be handicapped back to twenty-three yards as noted in the diagram.

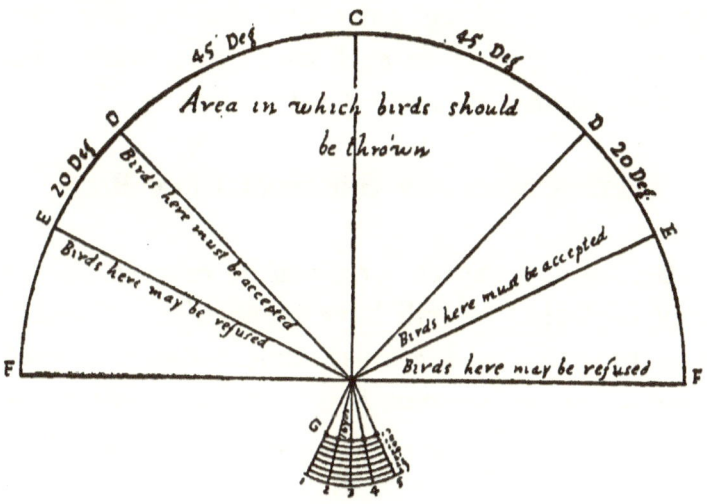

How Distance Handicaps May Be Measured at the Firing Points

Clubs containing a number of members, especially where their weekly or monthly program includes money or medal shoots, will find it necessary to adopt some sort of a handicap in order to equalize conditions and keep up interest among the weaker marksmen.

The handicap may take the shape of dead birds added to the score, or some similar scheme, but the best and most practical handicap is that of distance. The tyro should be placed on the sixteen yard line and others back of him until the strongest shot gets the limit of twenty-three yards where that is necessary—which will not be very often. It is not in human nature to go up against a losing game continually, and conditions must be made such as to give everyone a fighting chance of coming out on top.

INSTRUCTIONS FOR SHOOTING CLAY BIRDS

Before any expert form can be reached by the clay bird shot he will have to acquire a foundation of quick and regular time. Regularity of time is more important in artificial bird work than in any other branch of wing-shooting. Owing to its peculiarity of flight, starting very rapidly and quickly losing momentum, together with its natural rise and fall, there can be no uniformity of lead and holding unless the target is caught at just about one point in its course, which point must not be allowed to vary. The man who breaks one bird within forty-five feet of the trap, while permitting the next one to get seventy-five feet away, is certain of many ciphers on the score board.

A trained trap shot will break bird after bird

at any given angle within five feet of the same spot; indeed, he appears to be hitting them at one precise time from which he hardly varies a foot. The logical necessity for this becomes apparent as soon as we begin studying the flight of artificial targets. The bird starts from a position at the ground and rises so rapidly that at ten yards from the trap it is from six to twelve feet high. It continues to rise but at a slower rate as it loses momentum, until a point is reached where it begins to fall. From this it is evident that if the aim is caught close to the trap the charge must be sent high, farther out the hold might be dead on, and later still, below the bird.

The gunner's natural disposition, whether he is phlegmatic or nervous, will obviously govern his time to some extent, and experience will best teach him at what point he is most certain of his target, but when he has settled upon this spot he should stick to it. Above all, beware of the change of time that comes from overcautiousness, overanxiety, or that sheer nervousness that forces a man to cut loose without an aim. So long as a marksman can be rattled into changing his time he will never be a reliable shot. The fault to be the most carefully guarded against, however, is slowing up in an attempt to make sure of a bird at the wind up of what threatens to be a winning score. The best advice I could give an amateur when he finds himself growing anxious, slowing up, is to quit thinking, crack away, and don't give a hang. Never stop to blame yourself for misses and they will not occur half as often.

The need of fast as well as regular time can readily be proved. A clay bird which is strongly thrown is supposed to leave the trap with an initial velocity of one hundred and fifty feet a second. The bird loses momentum rapidly, but in one second it should fly seventy-five feet. Seventy-five feet is twenty-five yards, and this added to the sixteen yards which the marksman is back of the trap would put the target approximately forty yards from the gun when it is broken. The sharp edge of a clay bird is a pretty small mark to be hit with absolute certainty by the pattern of a shotgun at distances above forty yards; permitting the target to fly farther than this is quite certain to lead to misses through holes in the pattern; even the suspicion that that might be the case is inimical to good work. We may therefore conclude that one second of time consumed in aiming is the limit, and preferably the trigger should be pulled considerably quicker.

The man who shoots in one second can break

CLAY BIRD SHOOTING 151

a great many birds, but under some conditions of wind, weather, and strong, low-throwing traps he will find himself too slow. Indeed, with gun to the shoulder and birds going from known traps at known angles, the quick shot should be able to cover his bird in half a second. Even with unknown angles but known traps, the usual style, he should fire in three-fourths of a second which should catch the fastest birds inside forty yards. I have never yet seen a trap shot that I thought was too quick, always provided he shot with an aim, but on the other hand seventy-five per cent. of amateur shooters are too slow.

Naturally, if this quick and regular time is to be acquired, there must be no poking or pottering or hesitation to make sure of the aim. When the bird is sprung the gun should obviously be pointed beneath it somewhere so as not to obstruct the view. The instant the target is seen bring the piece up sharply to cover it, make your allowance for lead the moment the bird appears and you note its angle of flight; when the muzzle rises high enough, fire, regardless of whether you are off or on. If you lack mechanical ability to place the charge to the spot where you know it should go, that is something to be amended by practice and not by dwelling upon the aim. If by hesitation and a second aim to correct the first you should get your bird, the pottering would shortly become habitual with the certain result of never acquiring proficiency at this game. With the birds thrown as they are according to trap shooting rules, no great allowance for lead is necessary as compared with wildfowl shooting, but the problems to be mastered are rather those of mechanical accuracy in gun-pointing and quickness and regularity of time.

A further important reason for quickness of time in clay bird shooting is their flight characteristics. The targets are light and very easily affected by the wind; the longer the flight the greater the wind drift, as a matter of course. Moreover, the flight of a clay bird is something in the nature of the chips you used to sail when a boy. You could start them pretty straight and for a time they would maintain the line, but with loss of velocity their movements became too erratic to be foreseen.

In the same way, for the first twenty yards a clay bird seems to fly almost as straight as a bullet, then the air begins to influence it, causing swerves, dips, and jumps that the wisest judgment cannot anticipate or make allowance for. My advice would be always to catch your bird within fifty or sixty feet of the trap if you can; if you cannot, then quicken your time, no matter if you lose birds by doing so. Both the needs of shotgun pattern and the necessity of catching the target while it is in regular flight necessitate quick time.

In giving instructions for clay bird shooting many emphasize the importance of calculating the effect of a stiff wind in drifting the shot charge, stating that the pellets are often drifted three feet or more. Perhaps this is true in long shots, though it has always seemed to me that the target being subject to the influence of the same breeze would drift more than the pellets of shot. In any event, the best way to beat the wind is to quicken time, getting onto your bird within thirty-three yards if you can. Don't handicap yourself by allowing the wind to blow on you or your bird or your shot charge a moment longer than you are obliged to.

In time every trap shot develops a style best adapted to his own individuality. No man can excel another purely by imitating him. Nevertheless the novice can acquire many valuable hints by watching the work of a veteran. One thing almost anyone ought to be able to do and that is to see the faults of the other fellow. One of these, common to even many expert shots, is leaning away over the gun in a stiff, strained, unnatural attitude, which adds nothing to a man's control over his weapon and detracts from grace and endurance.

The 12 gauge gun weighing between seven and a half and eight pounds is the generally accepted trap gun. It should be full choked and should make the evenest possible pattern with 3 1-4 drams of powder and an ounce and a fourth of 7 1-2 chilled shot. Whether the arm is to be a double barrel, single barrel, repeater, or automatic is much a matter of personal preference. Long barrels are much favored, while the stock should be a trifle longer than for field work and straight enough to throw the center of charge twenty inches above the point of aim at forty yards.

CHAPTER IX

FIELD ETIQUETTE

I AM aware that in writing of field etiquette the chapter must have a didactic ring with its consequent dullness. My advice, therefore, to all who are fully acquainted with the unwritten laws that govern the sportsman on field and marsh, is to " cut this out." However, I do not feel that it would be right to close this book without a word on the subject, for there are two classes that I wish to reach, the novice who thinks he is privileged to shoot at everything that moves, saving only those guides who wear red caps, and the veteran shot who thinks that he *must* make a bag.

There is no place where the golden rule can be better applied than in the shooting field. If we govern ourselves by this old precept in the treatment of our fellows and apply the principles of a " square deal " to shooting the game, there need be little fear of any hunter forfeiting the title of sportsman.

Some wise man has said that every man is a barbarian at heart and only a gentleman from policy. There is just enough truth in this to make the saying disagreeable. Whatever he may be by nature, military discipline gives to every soldier the semblance of a brave man, the needs of business and civilization force us all to masquerade in garments of courtesy, the one suit much like another, but a man's true nature shows through his hunting clothes, and it has been aptly said that you never know even a friend until you have gone camping with him a week. Certainly pursuing wild things is an elementary sport, and the elementary in us is liable to be thrown into relief, betraying qualities good and bad that were never seen before.

Too many men afield are governed by the idea that it is everyone for himself and the devil take the hindmost. Put them in a pen and they will have the biggest ear of corn, though they know that in the nature of things this will lead to their dining alone in future. Courtesy afield is bread cast upon the waters which will surely return, but many seem bent upon eating their own bread at the time, taking chances on picking up that of someone else as it comes back.

The absolutely selfish individual can get along nicely in all his shooting and fishing trips, with the greatest satisfaction to everybody, with the possible exception of himself, by going entirely alone. Should he need human companionship

FIELD ETIQUETTE

a darkey or well-trained English domestic will serve him best. He can then take the first shot at every bevy, and every bird that follows belongs to him; he can have the choice duck blind and all the decoys; the best boat or the only boat is his; he can have the snipe corner all to himself; there are none to question his superiority as a marksman, and paid servants will be more pliable than any good tempered friend whom he may draft for the purpose. Such a man will require no instructions in shooting etiquette or any other etiquette, for the uses of politeness are only to make companionship agreeable.

So far as the ethics of game shooting in a sportsmanlike manner are concerned, a few words on the subject will suffice. With the possible exception of the wild turkey, which should really be made the target for a rifle only, no game bird should ever be fired upon when not in full flight. This rule must never be broken under any circumstances except to finish a cripple. I have known men who considered themselves good sportsmen who would shoot a quail or a grouse out of a tree, though they would not fire upon him when on the ground. Their defense was that the bird had forfeited his life by taking to a tree and thus refusing them a fair shot. This is merely whipping the devil around the stump, and such hair splitters might be greatly tempted to take a pot-shot in the first place were no one present.

No more should a wild duck ever be killed upon the water or at rest, no matter how difficult the stalk or how scarce the birds may be. A bag of birds killed in any manner except fairly upon the wing must be regarded as having afforded absolutely no sport, as not a whit better than an utterly blank day. Indeed, the latter can bring no after regrets and the former surely should to every decent sportsman.

The only possible excuse for shooting a bird at rest is that we may feed our vanity by displaying him, or that he is actually needed to satisfy hunger—few modern sportsmen are going about hungry these days. If the bag is of prime importance, if it must be filled regardless of the laws of sport, there is nothing to be said further than that the man who so feels is purely a meat hunter. Let the conscience of a good sportsman govern your actions when out all alone where there can be no policeman to knock you over the head for a failure to consider the rights of others.

Rabbits should never be shot unless going full tilt, and squirrels are not a fair target for a shotgun, not even when running. For that matter, many hold that nothing wearing hair or fur should ever fall before a smooth bore, and they are not very far wrong either. The rifle is the proper arm for such game.

Shoot no immature birds in season or out, and never make a target of anything that is not recognized as game. The temptation to shoot small birds is great at times when the shooting is poor, but sportsmen will not do it.

In flight shooting wildfowl the greatest pleasure comes from selecting your bird and cutting him down stone dead. Flock shooting is permissable because sanctioned by custom, but there is no great satisfaction in letting go into the middle of a flock of ducks without aim, however many may be bagged. This is especially true of shooting shore birds which frequently fly slowly and in large bunches. Cripples should always be knocked over where at all possible before another shot is fired at the living birds. Taking wild shots that are admittedly beyond the range of the gun is unsportsmanlike, though nearly all of us must plead guilty to that.

Shooting in Company

Man is a gregarious animal, especially in his sports and games. Even the solemn individual who plays solitaire likes to have an audience to see whether he beats " bogy " or not. Few would enjoy shooting and tramping alone for many days in succession, yet to enjoy the company of another we must make ourselves agreeable. No rule of thumb will make a selfish man generous, but possibly a word of warning will prevent the novice from dropping into bad habits. Shooting I have found to develop three characteristics in a great many, hoggishness, jealousy, and envy, any one of which is liable to become a spoilsport.

If your friend is a better shot than you, keep your mind off it and do the best you can. Should you excel, then for sport's sake give him a show, for taking advantage of one who is weaker is not to be excused under any code of ethics.

There are two abominable fellows to shoot with, the man who is a good shot and thinks he must sustain his reputation at whatever cost, and the "claimer." Sometimes they are compounded in one, and the mixture makes a bitter dose. This man knocks down your bird as well as his own with the expressed fear that you might have missed. He takes all the singles for the same reason—"feared you might lose that fellow." He sends his friend around to beat the brush for him and drive the game out while he takes it in the open. His shooting companion always plays dog when one is needed; the chump invariably pulls the

FIELD ETIQUETTE

boat and he does the shooting. All the birds at which both fire are his because he never misses and you probably did. At the close of the day's shooting he counts your birds and his own with ill concealed triumph, and then goes away to tell of how thoroughly he bested you. Have none of him; he is playing you for a sucker, a foil to his vanity. While the individual illustrated is known to all and will be with us always, yet it is not necessary for the novice to pattern his behavior after him.

Such simple rules of procedure as I may give here are dictated by common sense and a proper regard for the rights of others. They are in such common observance among sportsmen that it might seem a waste of time to put them in type, but I have seen them violated so often that it is fair to assume that ignorance is as often to blame as selfishness.

Beginning with wild fowl, in duck shooting upon public waters, the first man out in the morning is entitled to choice of blinds, or his pick of location for a blind. He is then not to be interfered with either by another gun stopping near enough to scare his birds or by getting upon his line of flight. Wilfully spoiling the sport of another without benefitting himself is the game of a city tough or a country " rough neck." Of course this has no reference to the friends who may from choice shoot from the same or from adjacent blinds.

When two guns are shooting from the same hiding place the leader of an incoming flock of ducks should be given to the rear man who is also entitled to fire the first shot. If only one duck or a pair come in they belong to the man upon whose side they approach. If a flock of birds are passing, the gunner they reach last is entitled to give the word to fire. Should a pair of blinds be situated a short distance apart, as usually happens, one marksman must never be tempted to shoot at birds that are passing directly over the other gun until its owner has discharged both barrels. Few things are more provocative of ill feeling than to have one gun take birds that plainly belonged to the other, either killing them or driving them away. The shooter who will do this belongs to the impossible class—the go it alone and be hanged to them. Neither should a man call to birds that are evidently decoying to another.

Where two men are shooting from a boat, as in jumping ducks, the one pulling while the other handles the gun, nothing should tempt the oarsman to touch his gun—not even stopping cripples that are otherwise sure to escape. For the time his sole business is to manage the boat.

With a fixed time to begin and desist from shooting upon a marsh, whether the hour was set by law or a club, never fail to observe the rule to the minute. Should the gunner permit himself to be tempted into shooting previous to the prescribed time, he would be infringing upon the rights of others by starting the fowl to flying before the blinds had been occupied. Shooting after hours is also an unwarranted liberty as it may injure the sport of the following day.

If any man takes a bird that was undoubtedly yours, claim the fowl and place it in your bag; it may teach the selfish shooter a lesson.

In field shooting two are company and three a crowd, unless the trio of guns are very steady and accustomed to working together. More than three guns should never follow one brace of dogs.

When two men are shooting together, each over his own dog, the bird or shot belongs to the man whose dog found it, and his friend should never fire first unless invited to do so. It is nothing short of dishonesty to take the bird that has been found by the dog of another except with the owner's express permission. Should but one of the party own a dog the duties of a host fall upon him, requiring that he give his companion a fair share of the shooting.

In covey shooting an imaginary line should be kept in mind, the birds going to the right of this belonging to the gun on that side and all upon the other to the left gun. A disagreeable thing that will happen now and then is to have both guns discharged at one bird. This should occur but rarely if care is exercised not to shoot upon the wrong side of the line, and when it does the bird belongs to the man upon whose ground it has fallen.

The business of "wiping the eye" of another, as it is called, is not to be commended. The bird belongs to the man upon whose side it breaks until he has fired both barrels, and he should not be interfered with, hurried, or rattled by the fear of another charge cutting in. When he has finished shooting it will generally be too late for the second man to deliver a killing shot, and one that merely pricks or wounds is very unsportsmanlike. A continued and deliberate attempt to kill game that has been missed by another can only result in developing unpleasantness. Shooting at the bird of another before he has had time to fire both barrels is an indefensible proceeding.

The owner of the dog which is standing game has the right to point out the positions which other guns should occupy when the bevy breaks, but his duty as host would demand that he did

FIELD ETIQUETTE

not select the place of vantage for himself. If necessary for someone to walk the game up, he can delegate this duty to another or assume it himself. For the time being he is master of ceremonies.

In cover shooting, two guns hunting together should be the limit, and these must keep in close touch with one another. When of necessity they are forced to separate constant signals should be exchanged. The man who violates this rule endangers both himself and his companion. I can recall shooting quail with a friend in the hazel thickets of Illinois. We took separate paths and lost sight of one another for a few seconds. Looking down a hazel lane I saw my dog pointing. As I started for him a quail broke, taking a course straight for my head. I dodged and at the same time the other gun cracked, overshooting the bird and thus missing me. My companion violated two rules in thus shooting, flushing birds to the point of another's dog without permission and firing at all without absolutely knowing the whereabouts of the other gun.

In a nearly similar occurrence a fine young sportsman of St. Louis had both eyes shot out. Remember that there is little time to think after the game is on the wing so every precaution must be taken previous to flushing the bird, and the man who is willing to take the slightest chance of injuring another for the sake of shooting is a criminal in the guise of a sportsman.

I doubt if there is one experienced gunner who has not at some time or other had his ears split with the sharp crack of nitro powder. More than one gunner has had his hearing permanently injured by this fool's trick, and many a day has been spoiled by it. The author vividly remembers shooting with a man who was partially deaf, and who not being able to hear much himself was utterly reckless about other people's ears. When the gentleman did catch a sound it seemed that he heard it most plainly, and finally while he was busy aiming I let off my gun behind his head. The one lesson was enough.

When field shooting in a settled community, never fire a shot within less than forty rods of a house, or of people at work in the field. There may be ladies and children about the place who will be rendered nervous by the sound of a gun, and this will finally provoke the owner into forbidding all shooting. That express permission may have been given to shoot where you wished is all the more reason why the rights of the generous proprietor should be carefully guarded. For the same reason keep out of stock pastures and away from teams; half the ill will of farmers toward hunters is engendered by reckless shooting that might do damage.

In shooting by invitation over the lands or marshes of another, carefully obey the instructions of your host. Should he send you to a part of the estate where you know birds are scarce, go there and nowhere else. Neither go outside of the grounds he marks out for you, remembering that he and not you may be held responsible for your conduct in poaching on forbidden lands. In the same way accept the poorest duck blind without question or complaint, taking it for granted that your host is doing the best he can for you and that your time will come later. The position of host to a party of gunners is sufficiently trying without your adding to it by grumbling even to yourself.

A word now as to the manner of carrying and handling the gun: the one big thing to remember is never to point an unloaded gun at anything you have no private reasons for wishing to kill. Little need be said relative to carelessly handling loaded and cocked guns—they never kill anybody. The man who keeps forever covering you with the muzzle of his gun should be regarded simply as a vicious lunatic and proper precautions taken.

In the field three positions for carrying the gun are recognized as safe and good. The first is over the shoulder with the side of the stock resting upon it and the muzzle of the gun pointing upward; the second is over the hollow of the arm with the muzzle directed away from your companion; the third is under the right arm with the barrels pointed toward the ground. Carrying the arm across the back of the neck is unsafe and marks a rowdy with the same certainty as tilting the hat on the back of the head.

When walking up to a point, if on the left, hold the weapon across the body nearly at right angles with the muzzle a trifle high, but if on the right keep the piece directed straight out and down. A right and left handed man shoot together with greater ease and security than when both are right handed.

Here are just a few things to be remembered: It hurts just as much to be shot accidentally as with evil intent. You cannot impress anybody with your skill as a shot by beating him through unfair means. You cannot obtain a shooting reputation by telling people how well you have shot or can shoot. It is easy to see hoggishness in the other fellow and his eyes are as good as yours. Don't borrow a dog or a gun or loan either. Don't exceed the bag limit or shoot out of season. Stand for a "square deal" yourself and other people will see that you get it.

THE END

www.ingramcontent.com/pod-product-compliance
Lightning Source LLC
Chambersburg PA
CBHW031112080526
44587CB00011B/943